Soviet Aces
1939-45

SERIES EDITOR: TONY HOLMES

OSPREY AIRCRAFT OF THE ACES • 15

Soviet Aces 1939-45

Hugh Morgan

Front cover
Whilst supporting the final push towards Berlin in 1945, Lt Col S F Dolgushin of 156.IAP, 215 IAD, 8 IAK, claims yet another kill in his Lavochkin La-7 'White 93'. Despite attaining high rank and scoring 28 personal kills, Dolgushin had a rather chequered career. During the mid-war years, whilst serving as a senior member of the La-5/La-5FN-equipped 32.Gv.IAP, Dolgushin (along with fellow ace V Bobkov) was transferred to another unit as a disciplinary measure following a fishing expedition in which one of the regiment's pilots had drowned – 32.Gv.IAP's CO, Vasili Stalin (son of Joseph Stalin no less) was also removed from his post as a result of this incident
(*cover artwork by Iain Wyllie*)

First published in Great Britain in 1997 by Osprey, an imprint of Reed Books Limited, Michelin House, 81 Fulham Road, London SW3 6RB Auckland and Melbourne

ISBN 1 85532 632 9

Edited by Tony Holmes
Page design by TT Designs, T & S Truscott
Cover Artwork by Iain Wyllie
Aircraft Profiles by John Weal
Figure Artwork by Mike Chappell
Scale Drawings by Mark Styling
Printed in Hong Kong

EDITOR'S NOTE
To make this best-selling series as authoritative as possible, the editor would be extremely interested in hearing from any individual who may have relevant photographs, documentation or first-hand experiences relating to the elite pilots, and their aircraft, of the various theatres of war. Any material used will be fully credited to its original source. Please write to Tony Holmes at 1 Bradbourne Road, Sevenoaks, Kent, TN13 3PZ, Great Britain.

ACKNOWLEDGEMENTS
The author wishes to extend great appreciation to the following people who have provided advice, material or contacts: Andrei Alexandrov; Sergey Kul'baka; Alex Boyd; Nigel Eastaway; Carl-Fredrik Geust; Gunnedi Petrov; Professor John Erickson; Mark Sheppard; John Weal; and John Golley. Unless otherwise stated, all photographs published within this volume were sourced from the Russian Aviation Research Trust.

For a free catalogue of all books published by Osprey Aviation please write to:
Osprey Marketing, Reed Books, Michelin House, 81 Fulham Road, London SW3 6RB

CONTENTS

THE MAKING OF A FIGHTER ACE

During the 1930s, the exploits of Chkalov with his record breaking flights. the tremendous publicity given to the rescue of the *Chelyuskin* survivors (for which the Hero of the Soviet Union award was made for the very first time on 20 April 1934) and the examples set by epoch-making women aircrew like navigator (and later pilot) Marina Raskova all served to inspire volunteers to join the most glamorous of the armed services in the Union of Soviet State Republics – the Air Forces. In a public climate that thrived upon the exploits of its aviation heroes, and with the political will to develop a powerful air force, military aviation in the USSR did not suffer from a lack of volunteers.

Further, the political doctrine of collective responsibility lay behind the development of a range of activities, societies and clubs for the Soviet youth, who were channelled by the KomSoMol in the direction of 'volunteering' for future military service. Understandably, with the high profile of aviation, vast numbers moved into the air force.

If the activities of the party and state authorities was the spawning ground for future Soviet fighter pilots, then the OsoAviaKhim was the nurturing environment in which the great fighter aces were to cut their teeth. The training of Soviet fighter pilots of the VVS RKKA from the 1930s through the conflicts in Spain, China, Mongolia, Finland to the Great Patriotic War (GP War) was largely inspired by the massive effort of the OsoAviaKhim. Essentially a civilian operation, its formation could be traced back to 1925 when the ODVF (Society of Friends of the Air Fleet) amalgamated with the DobroKhim (Voluntary Society for Chemical Warfare) to become the AviaKhim. This was followed in 1927 by a further merger with the OSO (Society for Co-operation with Defence) to become the OsoAviaKhim.

This Red Air Force propaganda poster dates from 1937/38, and features the I-16. The Polikarpov fighter was christened the 'Rata' ('Rat') by the Nationalist Air Force in Spain during that country's civil war, and the description stuck and was duly adopted by the Lufwaffe in World War 2 (*via Seibel*)

The new organisation took eager young air-minded men and women and turned them into skilled aviation specialists, including aircrew. By the outset of the GP War, the OsoAviaKhim had helped at least 120,000 pilots – both men and women – obtain their civilian pilots licence, which was roughly equivalent to today's Private Pilot's Licence (PPL) in the UK.

This vast number of civilian-trained pilots provided a numerically strong reserve of pilots for the Soviet Air Forces. However, in terms of quality, most pilots coming from the OsoAviaKhim were ill-prepared for military aviation and combat flying. It was true that some had managed to log several thousand hours of flying time as instructors, but in the main, the OsoAviaKhim pilot training programme provided the VVS with large quantities of pilots insufficiently prepared to quickly match the skilled *Jagdflieger* of the Luftwaffe.

Pilots posted in to fighter regiments in 1941 could expect very little guidance in combat techniques or aerial gunnery, the operational focus being placed instead on formation flying - the harsh lessons of Spain and Finland were largely ignored. Operational training was therefore woefully inadequate inlight of what was soon to be unleashed on the VVS from the west, and this situation did not improve until successful fighter leaders gained the opportunity to impart their personal knowledge of fighter combat to their tactically innocent colleagues in 1942.

THE FIRST ACES

Reeling from the decimation inflicted by the German *blitzkrieg* which commenced on 22 June 1941, those Soviet fighter pilots that managed to survive the horrendous losses through a combination of sheer luck and raw skill soon began to work up good scores – there was certainly no shortage of Luftwaffe targets that first bloody summer on the Eastern Front. These successes provided the only 'good' war news for the oppressed and anxious Soviet public, and the highest scoring pilots were quickly identified in political circles by those who saw the massive potential to boost public morale through the creation of heroes. In December 1941 the term 'ace' was officially used for the first time to describe pilots with three or more confirmed combat kills, these men usually being given the opportunity to describe their achievements in the form of written articles by ghost writers published in Party papers like *Pravda*. Aces were also permitted to adorn their aircraft with personal markings

By the end of 1942 Gen T T Khryukin raised the score pilots had to achieve to earn ace status to at least ten enemy aircraft destroyed. Those who succeeded in matching the new criterion became associated with the highest military decoration that the USSR could bestow, the Gold Star of the Hero of the Soviet Union (HSU), which was automatically awarded to any pilot after he or she had downed ten aircraft.

Posters on display urged the populace to follow the example of the 'aces', with recipients of the Gold Star often being individually named. Top 'aces' like Pokryshkin, Rechkalov and Kozhedub soon became household names, and their exploits have since merged into folklore.

A typical ace of the early war period would have inevitably been a young KomSoMol member who had learned to fly in an OsoAviaKhim aeroclub in the late 1930s. He would have then graduated to a military training school as a VVS pilot just after the outbreak of war, eventually becoming

This 1942 vintage propaganda poster extols the potency of Stalin's 'Falcons' – in this case MiG-3s ripping into a Luftwaffe 'Vulture'. In reality the MiG-3 proved to be largely unsuccessful when used as a fighter against the *Jagdwaffe*, and it was eventually relegated to tactical reconnaissance duties following its participation in the defence of Moscow (*via Seibel*)

This 1945 period poster glorifies the 'heavenly' virtues of the Yak stable of fighters (*via Seibel*)

an instructor before finally entering the fray in the spring of 1943. Examples of such aces include Ivan Kozhedub (the highest scoring Allied pilot of World War 2 with 62 kills), Kirill Yevstigeyev, who was credited with 53 kills, and Vladimir Lavrinyenkov who downed 23 enemy aircraft. Most, but not all, would be Party members.

Those former cadet pilots fortunate enough to end up in a leading fighter regiment, and who displayed good innate abilities and received guidance from an experienced and capable 'teacher', usually went on to amass a reasonable score by the conclusion of the war.

COMBAT CLAIMS

In the study of the methods by which combat claims were recognised by higher authorities, the VVS provides a particularly fascinating and unique example. Claim submission by Soviet fighter pilots was comparable with their counterparts in other Allied and Axis air forces, but what really differed was the formal recognition that was given to the higher achieving combat pilots. Indeed, this acknowledgement of success was not only enjoyed by fighter pilots, whose exploits were easily identified by the Soviet public, but also by airmen and women involved in other forms of operational flying like ground attack, reconnaissance and bombing.

Commanders of squadrons and regiments whose pilots had achieved designated operational targets were also rewarded, as were technical personnel and groundcrews who, regardless of their 'trade', were eligible for awards based on the serviceability record of the aircraft they worked on.

Returning to combat claim submissions, and their recognition by the VVS, Soviet ace Col Vladimir A Orekhov, who was credited with 19 personal and 3 group kills, described the process in an interview conducted by Sergey Kul'baka in Minsk in 1995;

'After the mission, pilots gathered together and everyone spoke about how many aircraft they had shot down personally, and about those shot down by comrades that they had individually observed. The squadron

A Baltic Fleet I-16 pilot shows his groundcrewman the damage caused to his fighter by the Luftwaffe during a recent sortie. The I-16 *Tip* 10 was equipped with two synchronised ShKAS machine guns in the nose and a further pair mounted in the wings. The later *Tip* 17 replaced the nose guns with a 20 mm ShVAK cannon, and this variant first saw service against the Japanese in the Khalkin-Gol conflict

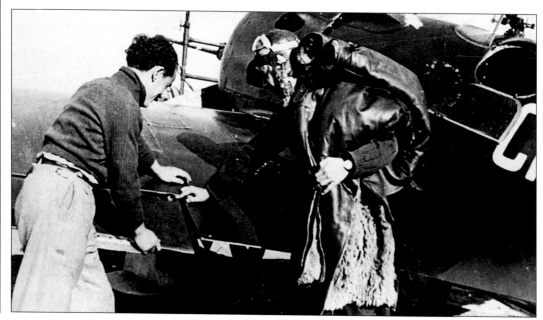

This photo again shows a Baltic Fleet I-16, but in more peaceful pre-war days. The first I-16s reached VVS squadrons in 1935, and soon claimed the lives of pilots inexperienced in handling the nimble monoplane – their previous mounts, the more sedate Polikarpov I-5 biplane and Tupolev I-7 sesquiplane, were for the most part viceless. However, with the eradiction of some of the handling vagaries of the I-16 by the manufacturer, VVS pilots soon felt at home in the stubby fighter. The latter's reputation amongst frontline flyers was further improved thanks to memorable aerobatic displays performed by test pilots Chkalov, Stefanovski and Suprun at VVS airfields in standard squadron aircraft

adjutant wrote down these facts. This document was named the "Combat Report of Fulfilled Mission". It had to be filled out after every mission, and contained data concerning the results of the mission, and pilots who claimed kills. At the end of the day all such reports were collected in the regiment headquarters, and the regiment's own combat report was then completed.

'The kills were usually confirmed by the commander of the regiment. To get a confirmation one of the following "proofs" had to be available:

1) confirmation from at least two other pilots who took part in the fight
2) confirmation from ground troops
3) confirmation from partisans
4) verification on the seized territory

'These forms of verification were equal, but sometimes – especially if the fight took place over enemy territory, and there were only two fighters involved – the last two "proofs" were obligatory.

'A confirmed kill was written into the pilot's flying log book, and this served as the official recognition of the victory. Confirmation took place on the same day, if there were enough witnesses, or after some weeks or even months if confirmation from partisans on the ground was needed. At the beginning of the war the process of verification was much simpler because the Red Army was in retreat, so confirmation by other pilots was considered to be enough. The practice of dividing claims between "personal" kills and "in group" victories depended on the traditions of the particular regiment. In 32. Gv.IAP (Guards Fighter Air Regiment), all the kills were "personal", and every aircraft shot down "belonged" solely to the pilot that brought it down.'

From this quote it can be deduced that the process of claim submission and verification was not especially contentious, pilots simply requiring evidence from a corroborating source in order to support their claims – as was the case with most other wartime combatants. Certainly this was the situation during the GP War, although scores accrued by Soviet pilots during the earlier 'Winter War' with Finland, as well as those that saw action in Spain and China during the late 1930s, are less easily substantiated due to the paucity of readily available records from these conflicts.

The problems posed by the lack of documentation from the Spanish Civil War are slightly eased by the fact that Republican units tended to accredit combat claims on a 'group' basis, rather than to an individual – thus reflecting the political ethos of collective ownership. However, in both the Nomonhan Incident on the Chinese/Mongolian border and the 'Winter War' with Finland, over-claiming by VVS pilots was rife. Indeed, kill accreditation in the latter conflict was so unrealistically high that it could be labelled outlandish, particularly when compared with the accurate records kept by the Finns pertaining to their own losses.

VVS groundcrews were eligible for awards which emphasised their technical proficiency and productivity. Like their flying colleagues, these men (and women) also received citations and medals in recognition of good work. Such awards helped foster a strong bond between fighter pilots and the groundcrews who serviced their aircraft. This undoubtedly posed shot shows personnel working out in the open on an I-16

When evaluating claims from the GP War, it became clear to the VVS high command that air-to-air kills needed to be verified by relevant intelligence reports, as well as by regimental commanders. Where air-to-ground attacks had occurred, then signed statements from the commander of the land forces in the vicinity near to where the action had taken place were essential. Finally, following ground strafing by fighter aircraft on enemy aerodromes, the success, or otherwise, of the sortie had to be supported by reconnaissance and/or intelligence reports.

In the case of 'taran' (the deliberate air-to-air ramming of an enemy aircraft), the claim needed to be supported by a written statement detailing the location of the likely crash site, which duly had to be confirmed by land commanders or by the regimental commander.

REWARDS

It was in the system of recognition and rewards during the GP War that Soviet fighter pilots differed from their counterparts in other air forces (with the exception of the Italian Aeronautica Nazionale Repubblicana, which belatedly introduced a financial incentive after its formation in late 1943). On 19 August 1941 Joseph Stalin issued Order No 0299 – official instructions regarding the rules used to govern the issuance of awards to aircrew of the Red Air Force in return for distinguished conduct.

Stalin's order from the Kremlin went as follows;

'I am issuing an order to introduce regulations in awarding the airmen for excellent effort, and to the commander and commissars of the aviation divisions to recommend these aircrew members for awards in accordance with this order.' His order system for fighter pilots can be essentially broken down out into the following parts;

1) *Air-to-Air Combat*

For every enemy aircraft shot down in air-to-air combat, a sum of 1000 roubles would be paid.

In addition to these financial rewards, the pilot would be recom-

Production of the I-153 'Chaika' ('Gull') commenced in 1939. The fighter was first tested in combat against the Japanese Nakajima Ki-27 over Khalkin-Gol, and although skilled I-153 pilots could usually escape the clutches of the agile enemy fighter, less experienced airmen fell as easy prey. As a result of combat in the Far East, the 'Chaika' was criticised by the VVS for lacking sufficient protective armour for both the pilot and the engine – many I-153s fell victim to accurate ground fire

Two I-16s patrol the vast plains of the Russian steppe just prior to the unleashing of Operation *Barbarossa*

mended for a 'government' award for shooting down three aircraft. A second 'government' award would automatically follow for downing a further trio of aircraft, before the pilot would finally be elligible for the higher award of the HSU after the destruction of his (or her) tenth kill. So, by the time a pilot had achieved this benchmark, he (or she) would have received 10,000 roubles and the USSR's highest military award.

The award of the HSU brought with it immediate public recognition, and for those 'heroes' who survived the war it brought protected prosperity from a grateful nation - for all its faults, the communist regime in the USSR looked after its heroes far better than most other Allied countries!

2) *Fighter aircraft involved on ground attack missions*

For a total of five ground attack sorties against enemy land forces the pilot would be awarded 1500 roubles, and for fifteen sorties 2000 Roubles would be paid, plus the recommendation for a 'government' award. For 25 sorties, a sum of 3000 roubles was on offer, as well as a second 'government' award. Finally, for anyone who managed to survive 40 sorties, or more, 5000 roubles was paid and the coveted HSU title bestowed upon the deserving recipient.

3) *Fighter aircraft involved in the attack of enemy aerodromes*

For four successful sorties in which aircraft were destroyed at an aerodrome, the fighter pilot would receive 1500 roubles.

For ten day or five night attacks, 2000 roubles and a 'government' award was presented. For 20 day or 10 night sorties, 3000 roubles and a second 'government' award was on offer, whilst a reward of 5000 rou-

bles and the title HSU was deemed appropriate for 35 day or 20 night sorties. Only missions deemed to have been successful through post-sortie debriefs counted towards awards.

At the time these 'bounties' were first granted in 1941/1942, 1000 roubles really did not buy a lot – a couple of good meals in a Moscow restaurant would have easily accounted for a fair chunk of this prize. A more effective (and no doubt more commonplace) way of spending the cash would have seen the aircrew bartering for goods, and thus ensuring an improved quality of existence. It is known that Soviet aircrew were particularly malnourished and given the food supplement known as KOLA.

Fighter squadrons constantly moved bases, living in the most primitive of conditions in often the worst weather conditions imaginable. Food nourishments became essential, and for the successful fighter pilot, any additional money enabling him or her to purchase a fulfilling meal was welcome, even if it was earned in the most dangerous way.

IMPROVED TACTICS

The influence of the 'Old Sweats' on combat tactics following the debacle of the early months of the GP War slowly began to be felt as the VVS entered its second year of war with the Luftwffe. Experienced pilots sought to remedy the wholly inadequate combat training by influencing instruction within operational units, and in late 1941/early 1942 leaders like Safanov and Savitsky gained reputations for teaching junior pilots.

Perhaps the finest example of them all, however, was triple HSU Aleksandr Pokryshkin, the third-highest scoring ace of the Red Air Force having been in combat since the first day of the German invasion. When instructing newly arrived pilots on combat tactics, he would fire hypothetical tactical questions at his pilots, and they would be required to work out the answers for themselves. Some 40 years later he recalled;

'In our free time I used to go through with our young pilots the actions fought by our fighter regiment, giving them concrete, basic, situations to think about, thus developing their tactical awareness and teaching them to analyse their own mistakes by themselves. Our dugout was often called "the classroom", "the air school" or even "the academy". Its walls were hung with diagrams, sketches and drawings, and there were models of both our aircraft and those of the enemy on the table. I should mention to that we prepared variations of previous combat missions, taking into account the different ways of engaging enemy fighters and bombers.'

Nonetheless, not all great VVS aces had Pokryshkin's ability to impart their experience and knowledge to new pilots. It is said that whilst Pokryshkin was a fine tactician and tutor, his wingman and long-term colleague in 16.Gv.IAP, Gregori Rechkalov (the second-highest scoring Soviet fighter pilot of the war), was far more of an individualist. He was not concerned about group tactics, but more about increasing his own personal score.

The correct loading of ammunition into magazines was crucial if pilots were not to experience gun jamming in combat

An I-16 *Tip* 10 of the Naval Air Forces is guided by a groundcrewman to its camouflaged dispersal area following the completion of a combat sortie. The I-16 was a familiar sight within Naval fighter regiments during the first years of the GP War as a vast number of Polikarpov fighters had been received from the VVS as the later force phased them out of service. The Naval air arm comprised four separate Air Forces, each of which was attached to a Naval Fleet – all four remained under the control of Lt Gen S F Zhavoronkov throughout World War 2

At the beginning of the GP War, Soviet fighter pilots flew slow, poorly-armed aircraft, and employed static and defensive tactics designed to provide maximum support to the ground forces. The tight, horizontal, three-aircraft formation, known as the 'zveno' was the dominant combat formation flown, and obsolescent I-15 and I-152 biplanes and I-16 monoplanes became easy prey for the German Bf 109s.

A defensive circling manoeuvre known as the 'krug samlotev' was used to provide mutual cover between VVS pilots, exploiting the virtues of the agile I-16 and I-153 fighters to the full. As Soviet fighter pilots quickly gained experience, so tactics altered to reflect the need for more aggressive counter-attacks to stem the Luftwaffe's domination of the Soviet skies.

Aside from poor tactics, VVS fighter pilots were also hampered by a lack of familiarity with their aircraft. For example, during the first 18 months of the GP War operational training on-type was limited to only an hour or two on the Yak 1 or LaGG-3, and pilots with ten hours on-type prior to gaining operational status were in the minority. Losses of new pilots on squadrons were unsurprisingly high, placing a great stress on the reserves of experienced men and women that survived this initial carnage.

This situation could not be allowed to last, so, running in parallel with the individual ad hoc teachings of those seasoned veterans at the front, considerable efforts were made by the VVS Air Staff to formerly improve overall combat efficiency. The Chief Administration for Operational Training, which came under the Chief of Air Staff, directed the formation of a unit staffed exclusively by outstanding fighter pilots who were then instructed to work with individual fighter divisions, or corps, in key sectors with a view to improving combat performance.

In February 1943 the group worked with the 256.IAD, attached to 15.VA, on the Bryansk Front. The following month the group was switched to 3.IAK, attached to 4.VA, in preparation for the Kuban air battles in the North Caucasus area. By May the unit had moved on to 2.IAK, attached to 5.VA, where they concentrated on ironing out the many problems associated with the introduction of the La-5 fighter to the frontline – they had to work swiftly as the unit was needed to play a pivotal part in the forthcoming Battle of Kursk, which erupted in July.

A manual of fighter combat tactics based on the group's previous 11 months' experience was duly produced at the end of 1943 in readiness for the air battles of the following year. At the training schools, the flying curriculum began to reflect the sense of urgency pervading frontline regiments, and aerobatic and gunnery training received greater emphasis.

The cornerstone around which these new tactics were based was the adoption of modern flight formations, Soviet pilots at last catching up with the other national air forces by flying in pairs. Pokryshkin, with the special permission of his regimental commander, was one of those who pioneered this formation in the VVS. The ace maintained to his death in 1985 that he was not unduly influenced by German fighter tactics.

On 14 September 1942 an order was issued to fighter divisions to establish pairs, or 'hunters', to patrol close to enemy aerodromes, and to pick off aircraft taking off or landing. Earlier that same summer the high speed vertical dive from height to attack the enemy had been used in action for the first time following an order issued on 17 June instructing VVS pilots to use height to advantage when engaging the Luftwaffe.

During the Battle of Kharkov in the summer of 1942, the 'etazherka' ('stack' or 'shelf') formation was born, this tactic seeing pairs of aircraft staggered in height and spacing – 16.Gv.IAP was the first to use this new technique. In the following passage, Pokryshkin describes the first time that he employed 'etazherka' over the Kuban during the spring of 1943;

'The regimental commander ordered me to lead a sortie of six fighters to clear the air space in which our bombers were operating. The group was composed of young pilots, so I also wanted the sortie to be an object lesson for them tactically. Having formed our "stack" of three pairs, we "combed through" the area where our bombers were at high speed. The pilots in my group kept a tight formation, following my every move. Me 109s appeared. "Let them be" I warned over the radio. I wanted every action to be as understandable as possible for the youngsters. Having let the Me 109s go past – they presented no threat to our bombers, which were still outside their zone of effective fire – I suddenly attacked the number one aircraft that comprised one of the leading enemy pairs with a "falcon blow" (a "falcon blow", christened "sokoliny udar" in Russian, was a surprise attack from a steep dive).

'His number two, seeing his leader's fighter burst into blue flames, deemed it prudent to retire. One of our pilots made an attempt to go after him, which, at first sight, seemed a legitimate desire. However, he soon remembered that only in extreme necessity, and only on my signal, did a number two pilot have the right to initiate combat, and he returned to his place. His task in this instance was to cover his number one, observe and evaluate the situation in the air, and be prepared for any attack.

'This combat discipline enabled our lesson to continue. A group of enemy fighters took up the pursuit of our bombers as they were drawing away from the target and closing in on us. It was impossible to wait as we had done before. I had to give the order "attack" over the radio. We dived down and the enemy broke. I brought down a number two and our second pair accounted for his number one. The object lesson had worked.

This flightline photo of 120.IAP PVO MiG-3s was taken on the day (7 March 1942) that the unit was awarded Guards status for its participation in the defence of Moscow – it duly became 12.Gv.IAP as a result of the decoration. The MiG-3's ability at high altitude made it a useful tactical reconnaissance aircraft, but at medium to low level it was no match for the Bf 109E/F

'It was important for our fliers not to miss a single moment of the dynamically changing picture of battle, which had for them a psychological meaning as well – a successful combat not only strengthened their faith in the power or our weaponry, but also created a confidence that the enemy could be successfully engaged. And for us leaders too it became apparent from the behaviour of the new pilots who would make number one and who would be better left for the time being as a number two.'

Other combat manoeuvres were also developed. Pokryshkin again;

'When we escorted bombers, our regiment practised a technique known as "nozhnitsy" ("scissors"). This essentially meant that a pair (or pairs) of fighters escorting bombers would alternate in flying towards and then away from each other so as not to lose speed, and thus giving each other mutual cover in the process. At the same time the pilots could keep a wide area of airspace in view. If you drew the flight pattern diagrammatically, it would look like a chain made up of figures of eight.

'When patrolling to give cover for troops, or carrying out sweeps ahead of our bombers, the entire group of fighters used a pendulum-like flight pattern known as "kacheli" ("the swing"). It was this application of new formations and new techniques of air combat which brought us victory.'

Perhaps the most desperate combat tactic employed by any air arm in the European war was the 'taran' ramming attack, initially adopted by the VVS in the dark days of 1941/42. Although this form of attack seemed to inspire admiration from the Soviet public, it did not always receive support for its use as a legitimate combat tactic by many leading fighter pilots.

Within the VVS, there were three main approaches to carrying out a 'taran' attack, these being;

1) To attack from the rear, probing the Soviet aircraft's propeller into the control surfaces of the enemy aircraft, which, with damage to rudder and/or elevator, would duly lose airworthiness and crash to the ground.

2) To ram a wing into the control surface of the enemy aircraft or, at low level, to tip the wing into the wing of the opponent so that he lost control.

3) To directly fly the aircraft into the enemy – this final tactic was used only as an extreme, and final, resort.

During the GP War, no less than 561 'taran' attacks were officially recorded as having been made by Soviet fighter pilots. Such tactics accounted for 272 German bombers, 312 fighters (both Luftwaffe and Finnish Air Force), 48 reconnaissance aeroplanes and 3 transport aircraft. One 'taran' was also claimed in 1945 by a VVS pilot operating against the Japanese. On 11 occasions, VVS pilots were recorded as being involved in 'taran' attacks against the Finnish Air Force, 6 Soviet fighter pilots dying in these actions. The first act of 'taran' occurred shortly after the start of Operation *Barbarossa* when, on 22 June 1941, Lt I I Ivanov lost his life after he rammed a He 111 with his I-16 – he was posthu-

With its propeller unscathed and undercarriage lowered, it is likely that this camouflaged MiG-3 was just one of the thousands of VVS aircraft destroyed on the ground by the Luftwaffe bombing onslaught unleashed in the first hours of *Barbarossa*

A rare example of early nose art on VVS aircraft is shown in this shot of a shark-mouthed LaGG-3 being run up prior to departing on a patrol over the frontline in late 1942

The La-5FN was one of the most effective fighters employed by the VVS during the GP War, some 9920 aircraft being built by Lavochkin between late 1942 and late 1944

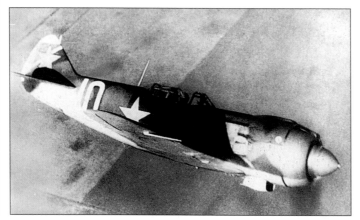

mously awarded the HSU for his ultimate sacrifice. The top scoring 'taran' pilot of the GP War was HSU winner Lt Boris Kobzan of 184.IAP, who attained an incredible four kills through the employment of this method, whilst fellow HSU Alexsandr Khlobystov of 147.IAP made three successful attacks.

By 1942 the Luftwaffe finally recognised that VVS pilots seemed to be seeking to ram their aircraft, this alarming tactic being alluded to in a document compiled by Air Command 3 on 2 October 1942;

'The opinion on parts of the Eastern Front seems to be that Russian fighters are starting attempts to ram our aircraft in order to make them crash. This view has up to now not been confirmed, either through the questioning of prisoners of war nor through the known Russian orders. It must be the case of inadequate experience or training. It has been shown that keeping calm in combat situations is the best solution. It is recommended that gunners hold their fire until the enemy is quite close.'

As mentioned earlier, 'taran' attacks proved popular with the Soviet public, who appreciated the aggressive and daring exploits of the likes of Victor Talalikhan of the 177.IAP PVO – on 6 August 1941, whilst flying an I-16 on a night patrol over Moscow, Talilikhan attacked a He 111 at approximately 15,000 ft, and despite being wounded by the gunner of the bomber, he survived the collision whilst the German crew did not. Nevertheless, several senior fighter leaders frowned upon its use, finding 'taran' an unnecessary risk. For example, Pokryshkin stated after the war;

'Personally, I was no adherent of ramming. In most cases it involved not only the destruction of the enemy aircraft, but also the loss of ours too, and not infrequently its pilot. If my memory serves me correctly, there was a special order issued by the Commander in Chief, Soviet Air Forces, Gen A A Novikov, in the autumn of 1944 that instructed us to explain to all flying personnel that Soviet fighters had powerful, up-to-date, armament, which surpassed in performance all enemy fighters currently in service, and thus making "taran" unnecessary. Ramming is one of the most complicated modes of attack, demanding great effort of will and the very highest moral and psychological qualities, and must be used only in exceptional circumstances, and as a last resort. Personally, I never once had to ram an enemy aircraft because I always had ammunition and my guns functioned perfectly.'

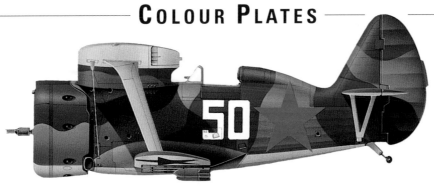

1
I-153 'White 50' flown by Capt A G Baturin, 71.IAP, KBF, Lavansaari, Gulf of Finland, Summer 1942

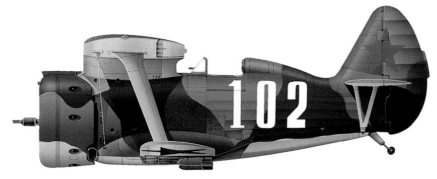

2
I-153 'White 102' flown by Maj P I Biskup, Commanding Officer of 71.IAP, KBF, Lavansaari, Gulf of Finland, August 1942

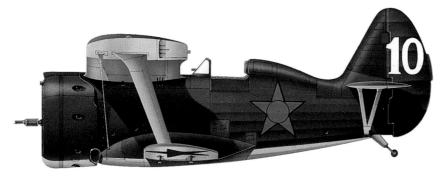

3
I-153 'White 10' flown by Lt V Redko, unknown KBF regiment, Gulf of Finland area, September 1941

4
I-153 'White 24' flown by Capt K V Solovyov of 71.IAP, KBF, Lavansaari, Gulf of Finland, August 1942

5
I-16 *Tip* 18 (mod) 'White 11' flown by Capt B F Safonov of 72.IAP, VVS, SF, Murmansk area, September 1941

6
I-16 *Tip* 18 'White 13' flown by Lt S Surzhenko, 72.IAP, VVS, SF, Murmansk area, Summer 1941

7
I-16 'White 16' flown by Snr Lt A G Lomokin of 21.IAP, KBF, Gulf of Finland, 1942

8
I-16 'White 28' flown by Snr Lt M Vasiliev of 4.IAP, VVS, KBF, Stalingrad Front, Spring 1942

9
MiG-3 'White 5' flown by A I Pokryskhin of 16.Gv.IAP, March 1942

10
MiG-3 'White 67' flown by A I Pokryshkin, 16.Gv.IAP, 216 IAD, Southern Front, Summer 1942

11
MiG-3 'White 04' flown by Capt S Polyakov of 7.IAP, Stalingrad Front, Summer 1941

12
MiG-3 'Black 7' flown by A V Shlopov, 6.IAP, 6 IAK PVO, Moscow, Winter 1941/42

13
LaGG-3 'White 76' flown by L A Gal'chenko of 145.IAP, Karelian Front, Autumn 1941

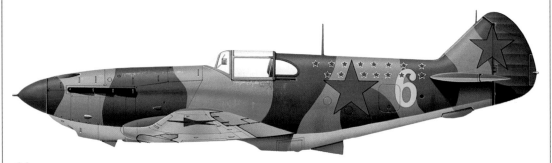

14
LaGG-3 'Yellow 6' flown by G A Grigor'yev, 178.IAP, 6 IAK PVO Moscow, November/December 1941

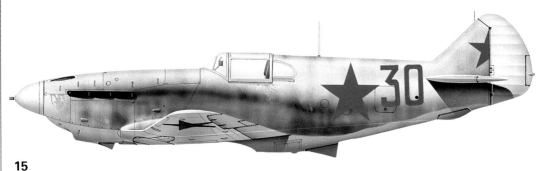

15
LaGG-3 'Red 30' flown by Capt S I Lvov, 3.Gv.IAP, Red Banner Baltic Fleet Air Force, Winter 1943

16
LaGG-3 'White 43' flown by Lt Y Shchipov, 9.IAP, Black Sea Fleet Air Force, Black Sea, Spring 1944

17
La-5 'White 15' flown by Capt G D Kostylev, 3.Gv.IAP, VVS, KBF, Leningrad, 1945

18
La-5 'White 75' flown by I N Kozhedub of 240.IAP, 302 IAD, 5 VA, Leningrad Front, early 1944

19
La-5FN 'White 14' flown by I N Kozhedub, 240.IAP, 302 IAD, 5 VA, Leningrad Front, April-June 1944

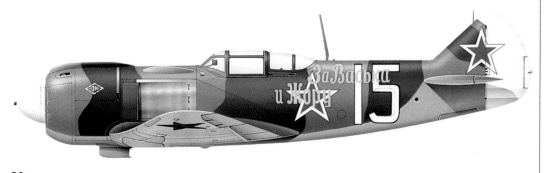

20
La-5FN 'White 15' flown by Capt P Ya Likholetov, 159.IAP, Leningrad, Summer 1944

21
La-5FN 'White 93' flown by Snr Lt V Orekhov, 32.Gv.IAP, 3 Gv.IAD, 1 Gv.IAK, Kursk, July 1943

22
La-5FN 'White 01' flown Capt V I Popkov of 5.Gv.IAP, 11 Gv.IAD, 2 Gv.Shak, 1st Ukrainian Front, 1943

23
La-7 'White 27' flown by I N Kozhedub, Deputy CO of 176.Gv.IAP, 302 IAD, Germany, Spring 1945

24
La-7 'White 93' flown by Lt Col S F Dolgushin, 156.IAP, 215 IAD, 8 IAK, Germany, 1945

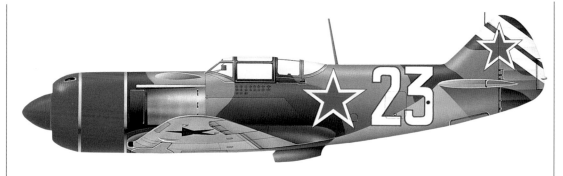

25
La-7 'White 23' flown by Maj V Orekhov, 32.Gv.IAP, 3 Gv.IAD, 1 Gv.IAK, Latvia, September 1944

26
Yak-1 'White 1' flown by Snr Lt M D Baranov, 183.IAP, Summer 1942

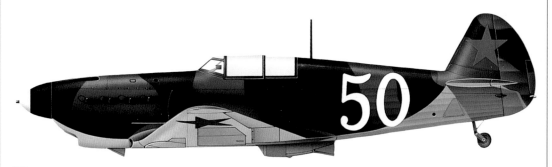

27
Yak-1 'White 50' flown by Lt Col V F Golubov, 18.Gv.IAP, Khationki, Spring 1943

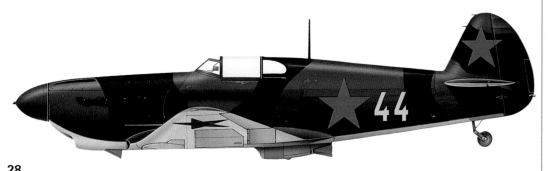

28
Yak-1 'Yellow 44' flown by Lilya Litvyak of 296.IAP, Stalingrad, Spring 1943

29
Yak-1 'White 58' flown by Capt S D Lugansky, 270.IAP, 203 IAD, 2nd Ukrainian Front, November 1943

30
Yak-1 (no number) flown by Maj A M Reshetov, 37.Gv.IAP, 6 Gv.IAD, 2nd Ukranian Front, 1943

31
Yak-1 (no number) flown by Maj B M Yeremin, 37.Gv.IAP, 6 Gv.IAD, 2nd Ukrainian Front, early 1943

32
Yak-7B 'White 31' flown by Snr Lt V Orekhov, 434.IAP, Stalingrad, September 1942

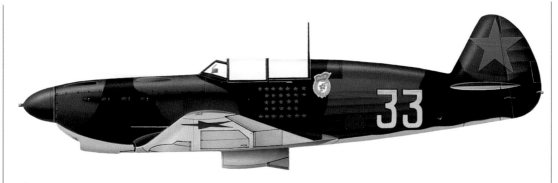

33
Yak-7B 'Yelow 33' flown by Maj P Pokryshev, 159.IAP, Leningrad Front, 1945

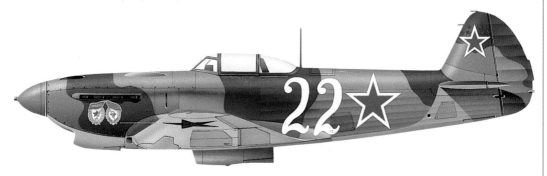

34
Yak-9D 'White 22' flown by Maj M Grib, 6.Gv.IAP, VVS ChF (Black Sea Fleet Air Force), May 1944

35
Yak-9T 'White 38' flown by Snr Lt A I Vybornov of 728.IAP, 256 IAD, southern Poland, late 1944

36
Yak-3 (no number) flown by Maj-Gen G Zakharov, 303 IAD, 1 VA, Lithuania, 1944

37
Yak-3 'White 5' flown by R Sauvage, *Normandie-Niemen Groupe,* 303 IAD, 1 VA, German Baltic Coast, March 1945

38
P-39Q Airacobra 44-2547 flown by Capt G A Rechkalov, 16.Gv.IAP, 9 Gv.IAD, 5 VA, Ukrainian Front, Summer 1944

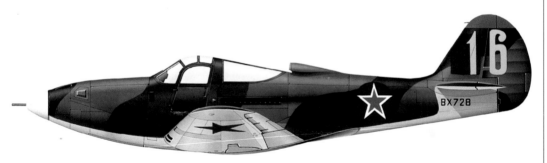

39
P-400 Airacobra BX728 'Yellow 16' flown by Capt I V Bochkov, 19.Gv.IAP, East Karelia, 1942

40
P-40K Warhawk 'White 23' flown by N F Kuznetsov, 436.IAP, Northern Fleet Air Force, circa 1942

1
Capt P J Likholetov of 159.IAP is seen
in the summer of 1944

2
Capt Boris F Safonov of 72.IAP (North
-ern Fleet Air Force), September 1941

3
Capt A V Alelyukhin of 9.Gv.IAP in
September 1943

4
Capt N A Zelenov of the Naval Air
Forces in 1942/43

5
Capt P I Chepinoga of 508.IAP in
November 1944

6
Capt I N Kozhedub of 176.Gv.IAP in
August 1944

EVOLUTION OF VVS FIGHTER AVIATION 1941-45

At 03.30 hours on the morning of Sunday, 22 June 1941, 10 Soviet forward area airfields were attacked by 30 Luftwaffe aircraft. These first raids by Do 17Zs, Ju 88s and He 111s took the VVS completely by surprise, and heralded the start of the heaviest *blitzkrieg* attack the world had ever seen. The warning signs had been clear since the early months of 1941, for the German build-up had started in the winter of 1940 and Luftwaffe reconnaissance flights over the Soviet Union had commenced in February 1941.

In his memoirs, Aleksandr Pokryshkin describes his increasing frustration at not being able to counter these recce flights, which he felt insulted the Soviet Air Force. Repeated warnings of an impending invasion had been given to Joseph Stalin by both the American and British governments, the latter issuing its final word of caution (by Sir Stafford Cripps) on 21 June 1941. Stalin read only political interference into these warnings, with the end result that the Soviet Union was ill-prepared for the onslaught that began just 24 hours later.

By the end of the first day no less than 66 Soviet airfields had been hit, upon which lay 75 per cent of the aircraft of the Soviet Air Force. VVS fighter defence to meet the incoming waves of Luftwaffe aircraft, which included 480 German fighters, was limited not only in numerical terms, but also by the sheer combat effectiveness of the pilots thrown into battle. The decimation suffered by the VVS during the first 24 hours was a portent of things to come.

By dusk on that first fateful day of Operation *Barbarossa*, Soviet *admitted* losses were 1136 aircraft,

This German photo claims to have captured the last moments of an I-153 as it flies through a terrific bombardment. The original caption stated that the aircraft exploded just a few seconds later (*BAK 781*)

of which only 336 had been downed during aerial combat – the bulk were destroyed on the ground. This figure had risen to 4017 aircraft by the end of the first week. The Luftwaffe controlled the air, and now looked forward to supporting the German ground armies as they marched eastward.

Faced with such catastrophic news emanating from the front, Soviet politicians in Moscow decided to focus on the few successes recorded by the VVS in order to try and boost public morale. Soviet fighter pilots had claimed 244 aircraft destroyed during the first 24 hours of the German *blitzkrieg*, yet the admitted losses by the Luftwaffe amounted to just 59 aircraft, a figure which had risen to 150 by the end of the first week.

During the initial waves of German attacks on the 22nd, 12.IAP at Boushev, near Stanislavov, lost 36 of its 66 I-153 biplanes fighters. However, many of the survivors made it into the air to confront the Ju 88s from KG 51, duly claiming eight bombers destroyed for the loss of three I-153s. The same *Kampfgeschwader* also raided the airfield where 149.IAP was based, and despite losing 21 of its MiG-3s, the unit managed to scramble a small number of fighters and rapidly claim the destruction of a further 8 Ju 88s. On each occasion, Luftwaffe admitted losses were not far short of Soviet claims, but this pattern was not repeated elsewhere.

Examples of overclaiming on this day include a pilot named Kalabushkin from 123.IAP, who claimed two Bf 109s, two Ju 88s and a He 111, whilst I I Drozdov of 127.IAP reported destroying five 'fascist' bombers during the course of four sorties flown near Brest – several others claimed multiple kills of enemy aircraft.

There were also 15 separate reports of Soviet pilots deliberately ramming Luftwaffe aircraft, the first documented 'taran' occurring at 04.25 hours – just 55 minutes after the Luftwaffe had commenced its bombing raids. The pilot involved in this action, I I Ivanov of 46.IAP, was killed when his I-16 hit his undisclosed opponent. He was posthumously awarded the HSU for his ultimate act of bravery. No less than eight 'taran' attacks were made on the first day of the GP War alone, this number

Taken just one day after the start of Operation *Barbarossa*, this German propaganda photo shows two obsolescent I-152s that fell into the hands of the Wehrmacht as it advanced into the USSR. Although the aircraft on the left appears to have been spared any damage during the capture of the anonymous airfield, the same cannot be said for its squadronmate (*BAK 77*)

The full horror of war is graphically illustrated by the burning remains of a VVS fighter, and its pilot. This photo was taken 24 hours after the invasion had commenced

including the kill scored by Lt D V Kokorev of 124.IAP, who rammed a Bf 110 over the Western Military District and survived to file his report.

Ultimately, however, any consolation derived by the Soviet leadership from these often hollow claims was intangible in the face of the military catastrophe that had ensued following the commencement of *Barbarossa*.

One of the pilots involved in the the carnage of the first 24 hours of war in the east was Aleksandr Pokryshkin, who was serving a senior lieutenant in the MiG-3-equipped 55.IAP, which had been temporarily located near the Romanian border in Moldavia. His first combat action resulted in him firing at a Soviet bomber and crippling the aircraft, before realising his mistake too late. This was an ignominious start to what became a glorious operational career, Pokryshkin eventually opening his scoring against the Germans the following day.

── SOVIET AIR POWER ON 22 JUNE 1941 ──

Even in the wake of greater access to Russian wartime documentation over the past five years, it is still difficult to assess the extent of Soviet air power on the eve of *Barbarossa*. In 1940, the USSR boasted the world's largest air force. However, in terms of fighters, some 75 per cent of them were outdated I-15, I-152 and I-153 biplanes and I-16 monoplanes.

The prototypes of these fighters had first flown back in the mid-1930s, and despite gaining many successes over Spain and China, the I-16 (which was the 'pick of the bunch' in terms of performance) was significantly inferior to the Luftwaffe's Bf 109E by mid-1941. The 'brave new world' of Soviet fighters in the MiG-3, Yak-1 and LaGG-3 had yet to be issued to frontline units in any great numerical strength, although by 22 June 1941 some 2030 of these types had been constructed.

By September 1941 Soviet aviation losses had reached an estimated 7500 aircraft. Despite such staggering numbers, considerable success had been claimed by Soviet fighter pilots – especially those operating over the Northern Front. The leading ace at the time was Lt P A Brinko of the Baltic Fleet, who had claimed 15 aircraft destroyed (including four Finnish Air Force fighters) within the first ten weeks of *Barbarossa* commencing. After being involved in near-constant action since the invasion, he was finally shot down and killed on 14 September.

A colleague of Brinko's from the defence of the Hanko peninsula was Capt A K Antonyenko, who, as deputy commander of 13.IAP, claimed 11 of his regiment's 34 kills before his death in action on 25 July 1941. Both pilots were posthumously awarded the HSU.

In the fighting over the central (and later northern) fronts, three of 29.IAP's pilots claimed 38 of the 50 enemy aircraft credited to the regiment as destroyed – many of these were for group rather than personal kills. This trio of ace pilots included Jnr Lt N Z Muravitsky, who claimed 12 victories, 9 of which were group kills, and he is also reported to have performed a 'taran' attack on 3 September. The other successful pilots of 29.IAP were Jnr Lt A V Popov with 14 kills and Lt N Morozov with 12, the former being killed on 3 September when he ploughed into Wehrmacht tanks during a sortie supporting Soviet infantry.

The first weeks following *Barbarossa* graphically illustrated not only the technical inferiority of VVS aircraft, but also the woefully inadequate training of its pilots. Both combined to expose the inadequacies of an organisation ruthlessly stripped of its best commanders during Stalin's purges of the late 1930s. Replacement aircraft and spares were soon at a premium as factories closed their assembly lines in preparation for relocation beyond the Ural Mountains – away from Hitler's immediate grasp.

This hardship soon manifested itself in a 'backs to the wall' mentality as the German forces closed on Moscow in their seemingly unstoppable march eastwards. The VVS were determined not to repeat their embarrassing performances of the first days of war in any battle for the capital. By late July 1941, Moscow was under critical threat as Smolensk fell and the German army strode through to the western perimeter of the city. Stalingrad to the north came under siege and Kiev to the south-west of Moscow fell, as did much of the Ukraine to the south.

A VVS airman lies dead by the propeller of his LaGG-3, the victim of a surprise attack by marauding Luftwaffe bombers on the first day of *Barbarossa*. The majority of Soviet fighter pilots killed or captured in the first 48 hours of the invasion never actually got airborne (*BAK 821*)

Hitler stalled from making an immediate onslaught on Moscow, however, so as to give his armies time to consolidate their positions at Stalingrad and in the Ukraine. This delay enabled the Soviets to organise the defence of the city, but also brought the dawn of the 'rasputitsa' (the rainy season), which beckoned the cruel winter a step closer. With the impending change in the weather, German forces would be isolated from access to the fundamentals of human life – warmth, shelter and food, and for military operations, supplies of equipment.

Under these conditions, the Soviet Union was in effect far better equipped for a defensive war than the Germans an offensive operation, despite the undisputed superiority of the latter's aircraft. Operation *Typhoon*, the German attack on Moscow, commenced on 30 September 1941.

Col Gen P F Zhigarev, commander of the VVS, held in his grasp the knowledge that his aircraft and pilots could operate from well established stations in and around Moscow. These airfields included the Central Aerodrome, as well as Khimki, Fili, Tushino and Vnukogo. In addition, Zhigarev's had at his disposal 6.IAK PVO (6 Air Defence Fighter Corps) of the Moscow Military Air Defence zone – this unit came to play a significant role in the Defence of Moscow. By contrast, following the first month of aerial and ground attack by the German forces, the 2nd Air Fleet of the Luftwaffe found the inclement weather conditions becoming increasingly worrying.

The advent of harsh winter conditions by mid-November rendered makeshift Luftwaffe airbases often inoperable. Groundcrews found their skin freezing to the metal surfaces of the aircraft they were servicing and repairing, whilst tools had to be heated with blow torches in order to allow them to be used. Liquid-cooled aeroplane engines also failed to start due to the extreme cold – Luftwaffe operations were being throttled by the weather rather than the VVS.

Unlike the Luftwaffe, Soviet air force operations increased in these con-

A *blitzkrieg* attack immediately following in the wake of the initial *Barbarossa* bombing raids accounted for the I-16 and I-153 seen in this German photo

ditions, the latter flying some 15,840 sorties in the three weeks from 15 November to 5 December – almost five times the volume of Luftwaffe activities over the same period. As the battle for Moscow continued, so the VVS began to rest control of the skies from the German Air Force. Under the skilled command of Gen S I Rudenko, the VVS counter-offensive in the north-west sector towards Rzher gained impetus, and Soviet fighters claimed 16 enemy aircraft destroyed.

A captured I-152 is examined by a Luftwaffe officer, who points out the hole made by shrapnel, or perhaps a machine gun bullet, to the cameraman (*BAK Loc 290*)

The activities of 6.IAK PVO became pivotal in the fighter defence of Moscow, and no less than 23 of its pilots were awarded the Gold Star of the HSU during the Battle for Moscow. The unit was commanded by Col I D Klimov until November 1941, when Col A I Mitenkov took charge. During the final two months of the year it claimed the destruction of 250 Luftwaffe aircraft in aerial combat. Further, during the five days of 9-14 December, 6.IAK PVO changed roles from fighter to ground attack, and duly harried and strafed the ground troops of the retreating German air armies, west of Moscow – by that stage, however, the corps had already distinguished itself in action.

Included in its number was Lt A N Katrich of 120.IAP PVO, who made the first successful high altitude 'taran'. Overall, 6.IAK PVO had proven to other Soviet fighter units that their opponents were not as invincible as they had first appeared back in the summer.

STALINGRAD

The battle for Stalingrad was really the catalyst for the start of VVS supremacy, with new organisational structures, new fighter aircraft equipped with radio and increasingly combat-skilled pilots creating the foundation for the change in Soviet fortune. Stalingrad preceded the successful Battle over the Kuban River in the spring 1943, followed soon after by the decisive Battle for Kursk.

There were two critical stages in the battle for Stalingrad, the first of which centred around the defense of the city. This was fought from July to the early winter months of 1942, and found the 102.IAD PVO, under the command of P S Stepanov, equipped with around 80 fighter types, almost all of which were obsolescent I-15s or the agile, but underpowered and outgunned, I-16. Stepanov appealed to VVS Commander Novikov (who was responsible for air force planning and operations) and to the Soviet Supreme High Command for the deployment of a fighter regiment equipped with Yak-1s to help stem the tide of Luftwaffe attacks on the city.

As Stepanov's supreme commander, Gen A A Novikov was a pioneer of Soviet military aviation, having earlier been personally responsible for creating a more co-ordinated relationship between the frontal air forces and the troops on the ground. he had achieved this through the introduction of the air armies, which had replaced the previously unwieldy VVS command structure. Fighter regiments had traditionally been used in a haphazard and uncoordinated way, resulting in poor operational efficiency.

Thanks to his grasp on modern aerial warfare, Novikov was readily responsive to Stepanov's plea for fighter support, and he duly ordered what has since been described as a 'crack' fighter regiment from Moscow to Stalingrad equipped with far better Yak-1s, -7bs and -9s.

VVS fighter losses were high during these early weeks and months as inexperienced fighter pilots were brought into to fly the new aircraft. Rudenko took stock of this and ordered his fighter regiments to refrain from engaging enemy fighters. A new VVS tactic was born known as the 'zasada', or 'ambush', which saw Soviet fighter pilots instructed to hunt and attack bombers and recce aircraft instead.

The traditional tactic of 'taran' was also effectively employed, and during five days in September, there were three such ramming attacks made – Yak-1 pilot I M Chumbarev of 237.IAD destroyed a Fw 189, V N Chenskiye of 283.IAD downed an undisclosed aircraft and L I Binov of 291.IAD was credited with a Bf 110. All three VVS pilots survived these ramming attacks.

The second stage of the Battle for Stalingrad commenced with the Soviet counter-offensive on 19 November 1942. Having attempted to stifle the air operations of the Luftwaffe during the defensive phase of the battle, the VVS went on the attack as the weather worsened on the Eastern Front. Fighter regiments began to assert themselves in force over the frontline whilst the Luftwaffe struggled to come to terms with the bitter cold. 16.,17. and 8.VAs, led by Generals Rudenko, S A Krasovsky and T T Khrukin respectively, made a slow start to the offensive due to the inclement weather, which had also severely affected the number of sorties flown by VVS regiments.

Although the MiG-3 was one of the newer types in service at the start of the German invasion (having first been delivered to the VVS in 1940), it too suffered heavily during *Barbarossa*. This particular aircraft was quickly knocked out of action in the first wave of strafing attacks that preceded the invasion. With the capture of the MiG's airfield just hours later, the forlorn fighter became the object of keen interest for the crew of a recently arrived Ju 88 (*BAK 389*)

Captured I-153s in various states of disrepair are huddled together on the corner of a captured field. Virtually all captured Soviet aircraft were unceremoniously scrapped by the Germans within weeks of the invasion

Rudenko's command included 220. and 283.IAD amongst its divisions, these two units being equipped with 125 fighters of which only 9 were outdated LaGG-3s. Over the next few weeks victories over the Luftwaffe were shared by the two VVS divisions, each claiming 33 kills for admitted losses of 35 fighters in total.

The German airlift of essential supplies to its beleaguered troops forced the Luftwaffe to commit large numbers of ponderous transport aircraft along the 200-mile corridor to Stalingrad. VVS fighter pilots soon learned that 'hunting' along the flight path within the corridor itself almost certainly guaranteed success, and they were further aided in their task by the provision of advance warning of incoming aircraft through the use of ground radar. The vulnerable Ju 52s, He 111s, Ju 90s, He 177s, Fw 200s and Ju 290s, whose crews included experienced instructors, were clinically 'cut to ribbons'.

As an example of the carnage reaped by VVS fighters during the ill-fated airlift, on 30 November 1942 a regiment from 283.IAD, led by Col Kitayev, attacked 17 Ju 52s and 4 escorting Bf 109s, shooting down 5 of the transports and 1 escorting fighter. Due to their sheer weight in numbers, Ju 52s generally took the full impact of the VVS fighter attacks during the air blockade, and by the end of the Battle of Stalingrad, an estimated 676 had been lost – around 63 per cent of the total Ju 52 strength committed to the campaign. Even the Il-2 *Stormovik* ground attack aircraft got in on the act, claiming a number of Ju 52s destroyed in aerial battles.

On 2 February the German 6th Army surrendered, and it was clear that after all the initial disappointments of the first 18 months of the GP War, the VVS was beginning to demonstrate the value of Novikov's new organisational structure, the effectiveness of the new Soviet fighters and the increasing efficiency of its pilots. During the eight weeks of the Soviet air blockade, the VVS claimed 162 German fighters, 227 bombers and 676 transport aircraft destroyed.

BATTLE OF
THE KUBAN RIVER

The 563-mile long Kuban River, running through the North Caucasus, was bordered on either side by critical Soviet oil fields, as well as significant deposits of raw materials such as copper, iron and gas. The Kuban was crucial to the Soviet war effort from both strategic and psychological standpoints, and as a result was also a prize highly coveted by the invading German armies. It duly became the backdrop for a bitterly contested series of air battles, during which several VVS fighter pilots achieved public prominence as a result of their high scores.

From the start, the opposition provided by the Luftwaffe was ominous, for the 4th Air Fleet (sent in to secure aerial supremacy) included *Gruppe* from both JGs 51 and 54. Both units were equipped with a mix of the latest versions of the Bf 109, the G-2/-4, as well as the Fw 190.

Their VVS fighter opponents could muster around 270 fighters out of a total number of about 1000 aircraft of all types devoted to the defence of the Kuban, a figure which roughly matched the Luftwaffe force committed. The VVS relied predominantly on lend-lease fighters throughout this campaign, the most popular with Soviet pilots being the P-39 Airacobra – the Spitfire Mk V and P-40 were found to be less successful, however. Although the P-39 had met with little success when in both USAAF and RAF service earlier in the war, VVS units flew the Bell fighter with great élan during the battle. Amongst the most successful exponents were Pokryshkin and his wingman Rechkalov, who served in 16.Gv.IAP – the former claimed 20 kills during the battle.

The first phase of the campaign saw German Ju 87s bomb the Myskhako beachhead with little resistance on 17 April 1943, but within three days VVS fighters were rushed to the area to try and stem the dive-bombers. Over the following week Soviet fighter pilots claimed 182 Luftwaffe aircraft destroyed, but at a considerable cost. Nevertheless, Soviet resistance was so stiff that the Wehrmacht was forced to abandon their offensive to take the Myskhako bridgehead.

The second phase of the battle was fought around the village of Krymskaya, which was of high strategic value due to its position north-west of Novorossish, and close to a key railway junction. By now outnumbered due to the overwhelming VVS force flung into the battle, the Luftwaffe lost on average 17 fighters a day up to 10 May – in total, some 368 German aircraft of all types were claimed by the VVS. The aerial skirmishes were far from one-sided, however, Luftwaffe fighter pilots exacting a heavy toll on their Soviet counterparts, who were frequently flying four to five sorties per day.

As mentioned earlier, much of the VVS hardware during the Kuban campaign had been supplied through lend-lease by the western Allies. One of the more disappointing types to see action was the Spitfire Mk V, which not only failed to live up to its reputation in RAF service, but was also often confused by VVS pilots with their arch foe, the Bf 109. Spitfire pilot A I Ivanov of 57.Gv.IAP explains;

'I attacked a fascist Ju 87 and was in a very favourable position, and probably should have been able to kill him. But alas, as if on order, our Yaks appeared. "Yashka! (Yaks !)" - I shouted in the radio. "Yasha! Don't

This photo of an anonymous *Normandie-Niemen* pilot was almost certainly taken at the end of the war, just prior to the French pilots flying their Yak-3s home from the USSR

disturb the attack! Give me cover." But our pilot apparently did not understand . . . His guns fire . . . My altitude is 2000m . . . My aircraft starts to rotate, the wing is broken, and glycol is coming from the engine cowling. I want to parachute out but the altitude is already low. I reduce the speed and somehow manage to pull the Spitfire out of the steep spin. I only just manage to fly home.

'The command decided to send us to all neighbouring aerodromes, in order to allow the pilots and anti-aircraft gunners to acquaint themselves with the English aircraft. Whilst touring of the aerodromes, I happened to meet the pilot who attacked and shot me down.'

By 9/10 May, the Luftwaffe had regained aerial control over Krymshaya. There followed a two-week lull before the Soviet offensive began in earnest on 26 May, with 4.VA bearing the brunt of the aerial fighting over what was christened, the 'Blue Line Sector' – the central section of the Kuban bridgehead. Reputations were made in the Kuban, and pilots other than Pokryshkin and Rechkalov came to prominence. Amongst this number were the brothers Dmitry and Boris Glinka, with 21 and 10 kills respectively, the former having achieved 10 of his victories in only 15 sorties.

Other pilots who scored freely included A L Prukozchikov with 20; I Fadeyev with 19; N K Navmchik with 16; N E Lavitsky with 15; D I Koval and V I Fedorenko with 13 each; and P M Berestnev with 12. By the end of June the Germans had been comprehensively defeated, and on 7 July Gen Novikov formally announced that the VVS had control of the skies over the Kuban.

BATTLE OF KURSK

The third, and final, phase of the German summer offensive commenced with Operation *Citadel* on 5 July 1943, the target being the Ukrainian city of Kursk. This battle was the final demonstration of just how far the VVS had come in developing combat awareness and discipline. During the Soviet counter-offensive from July through to the early autumn, several new Soviet aces had begun to emerge, the most notable of these being Lt K A Yestigneyev of 240.IAP, who claimed 12 kills in only 9 sorties and ended the war with 56 victories and two HSUs.

The four major battles for Moscow, Stalingrad, the Kuban and Kursk had seen the VVS RKKA transformed from an ill-coordinated, poorly resourced and under-skilled fighter arm, to a well organised and efficiently run operation, with experienced pilots flying modern aircraft which matched the best that the Luftwaffe could provide. The turning point in VVS fortunes having been reached, it was now up to the Red Army to push the German forces out of 'motherland' and press inexorably on to Berlin.

NORMANDIE NIEMEN GROUPE

Just a few days after Operation *Barbarossa*, the French Vichy government formally broke off relations with the USSR. In response, the Free French administration in exile in Britain offered to send a division of ground troops and a fighter group from the Middle-East to the Eastern Front. It eventually transpired that only the fighter *Groupe GC Normandie* was

transferred, which was subsequently expanded to become (by October 1944) the *Normandie Niemen Groupe*.

The first French volunteers to respond to the call for pilots to fight in the USSR gathered at a barracks in the English Midlands in mid-August 1942, before travelling to Scotland two weeks later to board the troopship *Highland Princess*, which was bound for Lagos, in Nigeria. Bearing in mind their future opponents, it is rather ironic that the volunteers were then transported across the vast African continent by ex-civilian Ju 52s to Rayak, where they met up with other French volunteers who had travelled from the Middle-East.

On 18 November 1942, the long journey by ship, air and finally lorry across the Persian desert culminated in a two-week stay in Tehran. At the end of the month, three Soviet transport aircraft arrived to take the 61 Frenchmen to Gurjev, circumventing the besieged Stalingrad on the way.

Although the unit was declared operational soon after its arrival in the USSR in late November 1942, it was not until the massive Red Army offensive in Central Russia in the spring of 1943 that the regiment finally scored its first aerial victories. Equipped with the excellent Yak-1, *GC Normandie* gained its premier kills on 5 April 1943 whilst flying from Polotriani-Zavod, south-west of Moscow. The French suffered their first losses just eight days later, however, when three pilots failed to return from an engagement with Fw 190s – three of the latter were claimed destroyed.

These first losses hit the French hard, and morale duly suffered. Its commandant, Maj J Tulasne, realised that his unit had to quickly get back into combat in order to offset this reversal with more victories, and the regiment was duly attached to Maj Goulobov's 18.Gv.IAP, where morale improved as it became more involved in the fighting. In May the unit commenced low-level ground attacks and quickly lost another pilot, but reinforcements arrived soon after – this was just as well as *GC Normandie* was down to only ten pilots.

The regiment was then attached to 303.IAD under the command of Spanish Civil War, Mongolia and Manchuria veteran, Gen Zakharov.

With its Cross of Lorraine clearly visible on its tail, this Yak-3 was one of a number used to great effect by the French in the last year of the war. *Normandie-Niemen* pilots greatly preferred the Yak-3 to either the Yak-1 or later Yak-9, and at the end of the war they were permitted to keep their Yak-3s by a grateful Soviet Union. They duly flew them home to France on 21 June 1945

Combat continued apace during the Battle for Orel, and from 10 to 14 July the regiment flew 112 operational sorties from their base at Kha-tionki, claiming 17 victories for the loss of 6 pilots, including Maj Tulasne – he was killed on 17 July when the nine Yak-1s he was leading as escorts for Il-2 *Stormoviks* were bounced by an overwhelming force of 30 Fw 190s. Tulasne was last spotted losing height during the combat, and he was never seen again. He had just been decorated with the Soviet Order of the War for the Fatherland.

Tulasne had been a popular leader due to his devotion to the unit, and legend has it that he regularly slept in a log-roofed shelter on the airfield just 20 yards from his aircraft. He had been credited with the destruction of two Fw 190s during the regiment's first campaign west of Moscow, and had previously seen considerable action with a Free French unit over Tunisia in 1942. Maj Tulasne was replaced by Maj P Pouyade. Also lost around this time was Capt Preziosi, who had earlier achieved the regiment's first combat success.

The start of August 1943 brought major changes to the regiment, which transferred to Smolensk in order to participate in the battle to retake Yelnya. As the new base was some 25 km behind the frontline, each squadron took it in turns to operate from a forward field just 5 km from the frontline. During the battle the French groundcrew was transferred back to the Middle East and replaced by over 700 VVS personnel, led by Capt Agavelian.

On 22 September 11 of the regiment's Yak-1s surprised a *Gruppe* of Ju 87 Stukas devoid of fighter escort, and quickly shot 9 of the near-defence-less dive-bombers down without loss. This engagement was the excep-

This superb flightline shot of Normandie-Niemen regiment Yak-3s was taken soon after the unit re-equipped with the new Yakovlev fighter in late July 1944. Note the aircraft above the airfield caught in the throes of a victory roll

tion, however, for during the fighting over Smolensk nine French pilots lost their lives and two others received serious injuries. In total, *GC Normandie*'s first campaign had realised claims for 72 aerial victories for the loss of 23 pilots.

With Maj Pouyade at its head, and a fair number of combats under its belt, the *Normandie* Fighter Air Regiment became a full fighter *Groupe* with four squadrons of Yak-9s soon after the fighting over Smolensk. During the previous winter, the regiment had received a visit from Free French leader Gen Charles De Gaulle, and with new pilots arriving from the Middle-East and France (the latter discreetly via Spain), the four component squadrons with the *Groupe* were christened 'Rouen', 'Le Havre', 'Cherbourg' and 'Caen'.

It had remained at the well-equipped airfield at Tula throughout the winter and spring, prior to leaving Tula for a new station at Dubrovka, situated between Smolensk and Vitebak, some 15 miles from the front-line. With the commencement of the great Soviet summer offensive in June 1944, the *Groupe* scored its first combat victories of the new campaign on 26 June 1944, but also suffered its first losses in the Borissov region. On 15 July the regiment was posted forward to Mikountani, in Lithuania, as the Soviet summer offensive pushed the German armies back some 400 kms to the west.

During the move to Lithuania the French pilots had carried their Russian crewchiefs in the fuselages of the Yak-9s, but a double tragedy occurred en route when Lt Maurice de Seynes tried to land his mechanically crippled fighter, rather than bale out, which would have meant certain death for his Russian passenger who was riding in aircraft tucked in just behind the pilot's seat. The fighter ploughed into the ground during the forced-landing, and de Seynes and crewchief Biezoloub were subsequently found dead in the wreckage. The unselfish action of de Seyne became legendary along the entire front, and further helped cement the bond between the French pilots and their VVS allies.

By the end of July the *Groupe* had received the order to move to Alitus on the banks of the river Niemen, where they took delivery of their first Yak-3s, which they quickly discovered were far more manoeuvrable than their battle-weary Yak-1s. During the early days of August the four squadrons were involved in intense combat, their stay at Alitus being doubly notable for the *Groupe* as they firstly celebrated the Free French liberation of Paris, and secondly received the accolade 'Niemen' by direct order of Stalin – granted in response to the unit's exertions in covering Soviet ground troops crossing the Niemen.

During early September *Normandie-Niemen* continued with its routine of ground attack missions, although pilots soon discovered that this was a task to which the Yak-3s were less suited than their earlier Yak-1s due to the former's susceptibility to being terminally damaged by light flak. From mid-September ground attack operations tapered off, being replaced instead by *Frie Jagd* (free-hunting) sweeps out of Antonous, although these met with little success. After a long spell of frontline flying, the longest-serving pilots within the *Groupe* were offered leave, but mindful of the forthcoming Soviet offensive against Koenigsberg (the state capital of East Prussia), all French pilots refused to a man to take their leave entitlement.

On 16 October the French-manned unit claimed 29 Luftwaffe aircraft destroyed, and by the end of that week, which had seen bitter fighting both in the air and on the ground, the *Groupe* had been credited with the destruction of 92 machines from 480 sorties – all without any losses! However, the serviceability of the Yak-3s had been adversely affected by the continual heavy fighting, hindering the *Groupe's* ability to perform to its fullest potential.

By the time the offensive ground to a halt on 28 October only a handful of Yak-3s remained airworthy. The following month Lt Roland de la Poype became the first of four French fighter pilots to be decorated with the top Soviet military award, the Gold Star of the Hero of the Soviet Union.

Gen de Gaulle made a state visit to Stalin in Moscow at this time, which coincided with the VVS transferring the *Normandie-Niemen Groupe* to the single forward landing ground captured by the Soviet forces on German soil, Gross-Kalweitschen. Blanketed in thick snow, the airfield was closed to all air traffic soon after the unit arrived, which meant that de Gaulle was unable to make the much-publicised visit to Gross-Kalweitschen. If the general couldn't visit his men, then his men would have to visit the general, so the *Groupe* was transferred to Moscow by special train on a journey that lasted two days.

Upon their arrival on 9 December, they paraded outside the French embassy before de Gaulle firstly decorated Soviet airmen with Free French service medals and then attached the 'Cross of Lorraine' to the *Groupe's* standard. Given three days leave in the wake of this ceremony, the pilots of the *Normandie Niemen Groupe* then made the long trek westward back to the front to start the final push into Germany – Maj Pouayde was replaced by Maj Delfino as the commanding officer of the *Groupe* at this juncture.

The third campaign involving the French unit lasted from January to May 1945, and for the most part saw them flying sorties over East Prussia and along the German Baltic coast. At the end of April the *Normandie Niemen Groupe* was joined by 13 new pilots at their Deutsch-Eylau base, although plans to use these men as the foundation for a second French *Groupe* – thus creating the Air Division 'France' – were soon shelved. With the war finally over soon after the arrival of the new personnel, the unit was ordered to return to Moscow.

Once back in the Soviet capital, the *Groupe* was told that they would be allowed to keep their Yak-3s in recognition of their contribution to winning the GP War.

These combat veterans were duly flown back to France, via Posen, Prague, Stuttgart and St Dizier in mid-June, finally entering French airspace on the 21st of that month – at 18.16 hours they flew at low-level along the Champs-Elysees. Just 24 minutes later the *Groupe* touched down at le Bourget to be met by the French Ministre de l'Air and the Soviet Ambassador ro France. They had arrived home!

A total of 95 pilots had flown with the *Normandie-Niemen* regiment during World War 2, 42 of whom lost their lives in combat, or were posted missing. Overall, the unit's pilots flew 5240 individual operational sorties, during which time they fought with enemy aircraft on 869 occasions, claiming 273 aerial victories as a result.

Despite the very temporary support of the RAF's No 151 Wing in the autumn of 1941, and the greater substance of the French *Normandie-Niemen Groupe* in 1943-45, the Soviet Union saw the political need to recruit foreign nationals and create national air forces which would remain under VVS control throughout the GP War. With a political eye cast over the future map of Europe in the wake of the defeat of Germany, the Soviet Union's recruitment of fervent and patriotic young pilots for the final invasions of Poland, Czechoslovakia, Romania, Hungary and Bulgaria made eminent sense both in the short and potentially longer term.

In July 1944, as the Red Army began its inexorable push towards Poland, fighter and bomber aircrew from the latter country were welcomed into Soviet VVS units in order to fly in combat alongside their Soviet comrades.

Soon new Polish-only units were formed by the VVS, with the Yak-1-equipped 1st Warsaw Fighter Air Regiment being the first of the Polish Fighter Divisions to see action. In December 1944 the Polish 4th Mixed Air Division was formed, which included in its composition the Ist Polish Fighter Regiment. A second Polish mixed air corps (the 1st), which included fighter, ground attack and bomber divisions, was soon created, and placed under the command of Gen F A Agal'stov. By the end of the war, Polish squadrons had flown over 5000 sorties against German occupied territory.

Czechoslovakian pilots also started flying in VVS squadrons in earlier 1944, before being brought together within a Czech fighter air regiment in July of that same year. This was then expanded into the Czech 1st Mixed Air Division, and thrust into the frontline over their homeland.

Similarly, Romanian pilots were also formed into a national Air Division by the Soviets, following Romania's newly forged alliance with the Soviet Union in 1944 in the wake of the shattered German-Romanian pact. The 1st Romanian Air Corps was attached to the 2nd Ukrainian Front to support the Soviet advance on the Romanian capital of Bucharest and into Transylvannia.

In Yugoslavia, Gen Tito's partisans were supported through the establishment of a special VVS unit which included the 236th Fighter Air Division, along with the 10th Guards Ground-Attack Air Division. Prior to the commencement of the final push to liberate the Balkans from German occupation, the Yugoslavian-manned 1st Fighter Air Regiment was formed. A substantial number of Bulgarian fighter pilots were also recruited in September 1944 to fight with the 17th Air Army, providing support to the 3rd Ukrainian Front's invasion of Bulgaria.

A Yak-3 of the Yugoslav-manned 1st Fighter Air Regiment is seen taxying over snowy ground in the Svene District in January 1945. Like other 'foreign' VVS regiments, which were staffed by Poles, Czechs, Romanians or Bulgarians, this unit remained strictly under the control of senior Soviet officers

FIGHTER AIRCRAFT AND THEIR ACES

As detailed earlier in this volume, the VVS was slow to adapt to the demands of aerial warfare during World War 2. The combined legacy of outdated fighter strategy, tactically inferior training opportunities for pilots, aged aircraft and Stalin's purges, which had extinguished the lives of many fine senior air force leaders and designers, placed the Soviet Union at a massive disadvantage firstly against the numerically inferior fighter force of Finland, and subsequently during the early months of the GP War. The road to achievement was tortuous, being shaped by politicians in the Kremlin who were essentially blind to the requirements of modern tactical air fighting.

The decision by the State Defence Committee to the transfer of all war industries beyond the Ural Mountains (way outside the range of German bombers) soon after the commencement of *Barbarossa* was to be the saviour of the embattled VVS. This massive undertaking involved over 10,000 workers, who were not only relocated, but were also forced to endure considerable hardship in their efforts to establish new production sites in record time. By 1942 these factories had begun churning out new fighter types including the Yak-1 and the LaGG-3, rather than the MiG-3, which had not proven to be a success at lower altitudes.

The harsh lessons of 1941/42 were quickly learnt by Soviet military and political leaders alike, and they rapidly turned to their most gifted designers to produce some of the best piston-engined fighters of their generation. By the last years of the war aircraft such as the La-7 and Yak-9 demonstrated the effectiveness of Soviet fighter design, and in the hands of skilled combat veterans, such aircraft proved to be deadly opponents for the Luftwaffe's Bf 109s and Fw 190s.

— BIPLANE FIGHTERS —

At the core of Soviet fighter aviation throughout the 1930s and into the first two years of the 1940s was the large fleet of agile, manoeuvrable, but increasingly outclassed, I-15 and I-15bis (I-152), biplane fighters, designed by the legendary Niko-

Two unidentified 'volunteer' Soviet pilots pose together for a series of propaganda photographs during the Spanish Civil War. The man on the right is wearing decorations denoting that he has been awarded the Order of the Red Banner (medal second from left) and the Order of Lenin (extreme left)

lai N Polikarpov. The ultimate biplane fighter from this design bureau was Aleksei Ya Shcherbakov's I-153, which refined the basic I-15 layout through the use of better aerodynamics – the fighter's 'gulled' upper wing and retractable undercarriage were the principal differences. The first production I-153s reached the frontline in the early spring of 1939.

The taller of the two pilots featured on page 44 is caught taking a photo himself. His wearing a weathered leather jacket not too dissimilar in style to the American A-2 of World War 2 fame

Four years prior to the that, the Soviets had achieved a major 'first' by introducing the world's first monoplane single-seat fighter into the frontline. The aircraft in question was the portly Polikarpov I-16, which quickly went on to win its 'battle spurs' during fighting both over Spain and Mongolia. The latter conflict in particular saw a considerable force of I-16s embroiled in huge dogfights (numbering up to 150 aircraft) with Japanese Army and Navy fighters as both sides attempted to secure control of the skies over the disputed Khalkin-Gol area.

Initially, the VVS RKKA fighter units fared well, but an increased force of Japanese fighters employing better tactics soon saw any initial successes eroded away (see Osprey volume *Aircraft of the Aces 13 Japanese Army Air Force Aces 1937-45* for more details). The Ki-27 in particular was much feared by the communist pilots, who began to question the ability of the Polikarpov fighter to match the Japanese machine. When flown by a

A handful of the 141 Soviet pilots and 2000 groundcrew posted to Spain in 1936 pose for the camera soon after their arrival. Commander of the air contingent was Yakov Smushkevich, who was to go on and make his reputation during the Civil War. On 28 May 1939 Smushkevich led a group of battle-hardened Spanish war veterans to Khalkin-Gol, and by September, had successfully pushed the Japanese out of the area. Stalin thought that Smushkevich was the ideal leader for the VVS during the so-called Winter War (the invasion of Finland), which commenced on 30 November 1939. However, his force suffered disastrous losses, and in April 1940 Smushkevich was replaced and duly executed on 28 October 1941 – yet another victim of Stalin's insatiable purges

This ex-Republican I-15 'Chato' ('Snub-Nose') survived the civil war to operate with the newly-created Spanish Air Force, who assigned it to Fighter Regiment 32 at San Javier

Boasting an unusual silver finish, this I-15 was adorned with a patriotic red flag on the port side of its fuselage, onto which had been painted the slogan 'For the Communist Party'. The fighter is seen here with its regular pilot, V Pavlov

skilled and experienced pilot, the I-16 could match any fighter encountered over Mongolia in a turning dogfight, but the former lost out both in terms of outright speed and firepower to the 'Nate' and the 'Claude', making it increasingly vulnerable to attack.

The same conclusions had been drawn in Spain where, initially at least, Republican I-15 *Chaika* had performed well against Nationalist Heinkel He 51 and Fiat CR.32/.42 biplanes. However, the introduction of Luftwaffe-flown Bf 109Ds as part of the *Condor Legion* caused a rapid re-thinking of Soviet fighter design. The most immediate result of this was the re-equipment of 40 I-15s in 1938 with the improved armament of two 12.7 mm BS machine guns in place of the almost useless quartet of 7.62 mm weapons previously fitted.

Soviet pilots were not only hamstrung by obsolescent aircraft, however, for their combat strategy was also well out of date by the start of *Barbarossa*. Fighter tactics employed by the VVS in the early months of the GP War had initially been formulated as far back as 1932 by the air forces high command, and these were fanatically adhered to until well into 1942. This doctrine basically espoused the need for a twin-pronged fighter force consisting of both monoplanes (I-16s) and biplanes (I-15s, I-152s and -153s), which would together engage enemy formations. The monoplanes, envisaged as high speed attackers, would either meet the enemy aircraft head-on harry them as they tried to escape. In direct contrast, the slower, but far more manoeuvrable, biplane fighters (which also had a rate of climb superior to their monoplane counterparts) would engage the enemy in close combat – essentially in the traditional dogfighting style of World War 1.

All fighter tactical training was focused on the co-ordinated action of the two types of fighters. Carefully planned, and orchestrated, rehearsals that involved hundreds of aircraft enabled tactical co-ordination to become finely tuned within VVS units. However, it took the unpredictability of war in both Spain and China to demonstrate that this strategy was seriously flawed, ripples from these failures being felt as far afield as Moscow.

The immediate effect of these reversals in combat was the calling of a meeting in the Kremlin in the autumn of 1937 to evaluate the painful experiences of Spain – both

leading fighter designers and senior air force officers were summoned to the capital. Joseph Stalin, a political leader who had a keen interest in the potential of air power, chaired the meeting himself. The final upshot of the conference was that N N Polikarpov was instructed to produce an updated version of the I-15 after both he and his project development leader, Aleksei Ya Shcherbakov, had argued that the biplane could still play a major role in contemporary fighter strategy. Thus the third variant of the *Chaika* was developed, being subsequently designated the I-153 – it was sometimes referred to as the I-15ter. A closer look at the I-153 is required :

I-153

Like the original I-15 (but unlike the I-15bis/I-152), the I-153 had the 'gulled' upper wing layout so loathed by pilots on the original Polikarpov biplane due to restricted visibility during take-off and landing. However, the design team went to great lengths to improve the pilot's all-round visibility with this revised machine, and few complaints were subsequently received on this score from the frontline. As mentioned earlier, the 'new' fighter also boasted a retractable undercarriage, and it has been documented that pilots used this feature to their advantage against their Japanese counterparts in 1939 in a most unusual way.

VVS pilots would deliberately fly their new I-153s with the undercar-

The gull-wing I-153 enjoyed some success against the Japanese over China and Khalkin-Gol, although the advent of monoplane fighters like the Ki-27, A5M and A6M2 soon eroded any advantage the Soviet pilots had previosly enjoyed over the frontline. This rare photograph was taken in China in 1939

This photo shows a 'war booty' I-153 on public display in Kaiserlauten, Germany, in late 1941. A number of captured Soviet aircraft were shipped back from the front for evaluation by the *Deutsche Versuchsanstalt für Lufthahrt* (Research Centre for Aviation) at Berlin-Aldershof

riage lowered so as to lure Ki-27 pilots into attacking what they thought were vulnerable, and considerably slower, I-15 fighters. Once the Japanese pilots had fallen into the trap, the communists would quickly retract the undercarriage, ram open the throttle and turn in to meet their foes. The VVS claimed that this tactic was used with great success during the first ever conflict involving I-153s, nine of the latter downing four Ki-27s without loss – the Soviet pilots involved in this action must had had well developed biceps, for the undercarriage of the I-153 was raised by means of a hand-crank!

Notwithstanding this somewhat dubious success, the I-153 was still stretched to effectively counter the threat posed by the Ki-27 and A5M, and with the limited introduction of pre-production A6M2 Zeros to the Chinese theatre in late 1939, both Polikarpov biplane and monoplane designs were decimated in combat by the highly manoeuvrable, long-range, 332-mph Mitsubishi naval fighter.

Although the I-153 was the only contemporary Polikarpov biplane fighter not to see action in Spain, it was extensively used throughout the short Winter War with Finland and during the initial stages of the German invasion (despite production having ceased in late 1940 after the 3437th example had been delivered). Whilst large numbers were destroyed during the Luftwaffe's initial *blitzkreig* attacks, many survived the onslaught to take the fight to the Luftwaffe, although once aloft they were soon downed by the Bf 109s they encountered.

Some pilots did, however, manage to achieve 'ace status' on the I-153, including two stalwart pilots from 71.IAP – Capt A G Baturin, who was decorated with the Gold Star in October 1942 after having gained nine kills, and Capt K V Solovyov, who became a HSU in August 1942 with five aerial victories. Their unit was operating over the Gulf of Finland during this period.

I-16

Polikarpov's revolutionary monoplane design first flew in the hands of Valeri Chkalov on 30 December 1933, and, over the next eight years, proved to be both a rugged and agile fighter. Despite these attributes, the I-16 was a difficult aircraft for novices to master, and many young Soviet pilots were to lose their lives in early attempts to fly it. In action in Spain and China, the I-16 initially performed with great success against the biplanes it encountered, but with the introduction of the Bf 109, Ki-27 and eventually the Zero, its pilots swiftly went from being the victors to the vanquished.

Yet, during the early days of the GP War the I-16 served its experienced pilots well when pitted against the might of the Luftwaffe. The diary of 131.IAP, for example, provides a graphic illustration of the successful employment of the I-16 in the six months following the commencement of *Barbarossa*. During this period the fighter was used by day to engage the incoming *Jagdwaffe* fighter forces, by night to counter nocturnal bombing raids, and as ground strafers in support of embattled Red Army troops.

Some 6016 sorties were flown by 131.IAP I-16 pilots, who claimed 68 enemy aircraft destroyed in aerial combat and a further 30 during ground strafing operations – in return, the unit lost 27 pilots and 43 aircraft. The

I-16s of 4.Gv.IAP, VVS, KBF (Red Banner Baltic Fleet) in 1942 are seen with their engines covered between sorties in an effort to fend off the cold. This regiment provided air cover for the vital Lake Ladoga to Stalingrad supply route

first claim for the destruction of an enemy aircraft was made 12 days after the German invasion by 2Lt D I Sigov, a veteran of the conflict in Khalkin-Gol, who, after being hastily scrambled from his base, attacked a pair of Ju 88s on approach to bomb Tiraspol. He gained altitude and came up behind one of the bombers, opening fire at close range and casuing a blaze when eventually resulted in its destruction. Sigov was later made a HSU, as was Maj I V Davidkov, who assumed command of the regiment on 31 October 1941 and remained in that position following the 131.IAP's receipt of Guards status of the VVS on 8 February 1943.

Other notable achievers with the I-16 were Boris Safonov of the Northern Fleet's 72.IAP, who subsequently became only the second Russian pilot to convert onto Hurricanes, and Snr Lt Mikhail J Vasiliev of 4 Gv.IAP, KBF. A second pilot from this unit to score heavily with the I-16 was Snr Lt Gennadi D Tsokolayev, who was awarded the HSU on 14 June 1942. Snr Lt Anatoli G Lomakin of 21.IAP, KBF, also received this honour largely as a result of his exploits with his personal I-16, coded 'white16', which was subsequently displayed in the Museum of Defence of Leningrad.

Some 13,500 I-16s were constructed by Polikarpov, making it the company's most successful design by some considerable margin. That it was still the VVS's most important fighter in 1941 can be gauged by the fact that the I-16 made up over 65 per cent of the entire Soviet fighter inventory on the eve of *Barbarossa*.

NEW GENERATION OF FIGHTERS

By June 1941 around ten per cent of all Soviet fighters were 'new generation' machines (namely the LaGG-3, Yak-1 and MiG-3), which had been in production for some six to seven months. These new designs had clearly arisen due to the glaring deficiencies that combat had exposed

49

within the Polikarpov stable of aircraft. The new teams of aircraft designers that had been formed in the aftermath of the 1937 Kremlin meeting
had been given the task of producing innovative designs for fighters in the
shortest possible time.

One of the design bureau (OKBs) established brought together the
gifted minds of A L Lavochkin, M I Gudkov and V P Gorbunov in September 1938 to build aircraft under the former's name. The first fighter
designed by this team was designated the I-22 (LaGG-1 in VVS service),
and a drastically improved version of this (known by Lavochkin as the I-
301) led to the development of the LaGG-3.

LaGG-3

Although ostensibly working for the same bureau, Lavochkin, Gudnov
and Gorbunov do not appear to have had an especially cohesive relationship at any point in their careers, and from the autumn of 1940 they were
geographically distant from each other. However, each was individually
responsible for independently engineering various marks of LaGG-3
between 1941-44.

Although the fighter had commenced series production in January
1941 in four production sites, its principle 'home' was at Gor'ky (now
Nizhny Novgorod), where Semyon Alexeyevich Lavochkin was based.
The original order issued by the Soviet government in late 1940 was for
805 LaGG-3s to be delivered for operational usage by 1 July 1941, but
due to production delays only 322 airframes found their way to the VVS
RKKA by the outbreak of the GP War.

Of plastic-impregnated wood (known as *delta drevesina*) construction,
and skinned with stressed bakelite plywood, the LaGG-3 was initially
powered by a single 1100-hp Klimov M-105P 12 cylinder liquid-cooled
engine and armed with three 12.7 mm Berezin UBS machine guns and
two 7.62 mm weapons. Early aircraft suffered from amateurish construction techniques which, combined with inherent design deficiencies such
as a poor power-to-weight ratio and heavy ailerons and elevators, made
the aircraft vulnerable in combat to both the Bf 109 and the Fw 190.

Lavochkin duly incurred Stalin's wrath when initial combat reports
returned from the front condemning his new fighter, and it was not until
the LaGG-3 airframe was equipped with the 1700 hp Shvetsov M-82
radial engine in late 1942 (the new fighter was designated the La-5) that
Stalin began to favour the bureau once again. The problems endured by
the VVS with early LaGG-3s stemmed not only from the aircraft itself,

LaGG-3 'White 24' (a 66th Series
machine) belongs to 9.IAP, VVS, ChF
(Black Sea Fleet), who operated
around Novorossijsh during the
spring of 1944. The 66th Series was
the last production version of the
type, and it introduced considerable
aerodynamic improvements over
earlier versions. Further identifying
features common to this version
were four exhaust stubs and a small
antenna mast. A 9.IAP LaGG-3 could
usually be distinguished by its
yellow-tipped tail fin and white
striped propeller blades, as perfectly
illustrated by this aircraft

This ex-524.IAP, VVS, LaGG-3 (35th Series) was captured by the Finns after its pilot had made a successful forced-landing on 14 September 1942 near Numoila. Although the fighter was damaged in the crash, the FAF soon had it repaired and repainted as LG-3. The Finns made significant use of captured Soviet aircraft due to their own acute shortage of fighters and bombers, often returning them to action against the Red Army. In fact, Wt Off E Koshinen claimed the destruction of a VVS LaGG-3 whilst at the controls of captured LaGG-3 LG-1 on 16 February 1944

Enjoying a brief respite from the near constant combat patrols, VVS pilots queue up for a hot meal served virtually under the nose of a LaGG-3 in mid-1943

but also from the inadequate conversion training syllabus devised by the air force to convert novice pilots onto type. Individuals could expect to receive just 20 hours of operational conversion training for the LaGG-3 in 1941 prior to being posted to an operational regiment. As if this was not bad enough, the LaGG-3 was often incorrectly maintained by front-line units, whose groundcrew struggled to come to terms with the temperamental Klimov engine. Indeed, morale was so low within units equipped with the fighter that it was whispered amongst air- and groundcrew alike that the type designation LaGG stood for 'Lakirovany Garantirovanny Grob', which translates into 'Varnished Guaranteed Coffin!'

HSU N Skoromokhov briefly remembered his early encounters with the Bf 109 whilst flying LaGG-3s with 31.IAP;

'Whilst the LaGG-3 had a similar armament to the Bf 109, it was slower, heavier and much less manoeuvrable.'

Despite relatively few LaGG-3s being in VVS service at the time of

Well-weathered LaGG-3 'Red 59' (35th Series) was regularly flown by HSU Kaberov of 3.Gv.IAP during the winter of 1942

the German invasion, within a matter of six months the type was being widely used on all operational fronts. Indeed, over the Kalinin Front the LaGG-3 comprised almost half the total Soviet fighter force.

Some heavy losses were suffered by LaGG-3s during 1941, although as pilots gained greater experience with the aircraft so the kill/loss ratios on type improved for the VVS. Better construction techniques also meant that fighters were being produced more rapidly by the New Year, and by mid-1942 an estimated 11.5 per cent of the VVS RKKA fighter force was comprised of LaGG-3s.

Notable aces who gained their 'battle spurs' with the fighter included double HSU V I Popkov, who was to eventually achieve 41 aerial victories, and Capt G A Grigor'yev of 178.IAP, who downed 15 enemy aircraft with the LaGG-3 during the defence of Moscow in 1941/42. Capt S I Lvov of 3 Gv.IAP, KBF, was awarded the HSU on 24 July 1943, having gained 6 personal and 22 shared kills with the LaGG-3, whilst Capt V P Mironov also became a HSU with 21 personal victories.

La-5

The improvement made to the LaGG-3 by the introduction of the M-82 radial engine was so great that it quickly won over previously sceptical pilots who had had to endure combat in the 'Lakirovany Garantirovanny Grob'. Initially dubbed the the LaG-5 or LaGG-3M-82, the La-5 had been initially tested in operational conditions over Stalingrad by a specially-formed trials regiment in September 1942. Pilots from the unit quickly ascertained that the handling characteristics of the new fighter were considerably better than those associated with the much-maligned LaGG-3, and the aircraft duly became the pick of the mid-war Soviet fighters. Along with the Yak-7B, the La-5FN was largely responsible for instilling in VVS fighter pilots a greater sense of self-confidence.

Some of the key VVS aces of the GP War flew the La-5 to great effect, including the most famous of all Soviet women fighter pilots, Lilya Litvyak of 437.IAP – she later moved on to Yak-1s with 287.IAD. Two HSU recipients, P I Likholetev, with 25 personal and 5 group kills, and Nikolai Zotov, with 28 and 10 respectively, both flew La-5s with 159.IAP. Ivan Kozhedub, the highest scoring Allied fighter pilot of World War 2 with 62 kills, also flew the La-5 and La-5FN before moving onto La-7s. Another high-scoring La-5FN pilot was double HSU Capt Vitali Popkov, who achieved the bulk of his 41 personal kills and at least 1 unit victory with the La-5.

Although perhaps not the most successful pilot to see combat in the La-5 in terms of aerial victories, Yevgeni Yakovlevich ('Ye Ya') Savitsky, ended up as the most senior within the air force when he was made Marshal of Aviation in 1961. This was quite a rise for a man who had spent his childhood in NKVD orphan-

The La-5FN (coded 'White 15') providing the backdrop for this shot was the personal mount of HSU recipient Capt P Ya Likholetev, who scored 25 personal and 5 group kills during his operational career. The inscription on its fuselage reads 'for Vasyok ('Basil') and Zhora ('George')'. Following in the wake of Pokryshkin's impromptu 'tutorials' with his junior pilots, a senior officer with 159.IAP holds a seminar at an airfield near Leningrad during the summer of 1944

La-5 'White 66' of 159.IAP is seen in Karelia during the summer of 1944. The inscription on its fuselage both praises the great pre-war aviator Valeri Chkalov and acknowledges that the Lavochkin was donated to the VVS by the Kolkhoz workers of Gorki

A flightline of formidable La-5FNs are prepared for patrol in late 1944. Many pilots achieved ace status flying this version of Lavochkin's radial-engined masterpiece, including G P Kuz'min of 239.IAP, I P Pavlov of 137.Gv.IAP and HSU Kravtsov of 3.Gv.IAP, VVS, KBF

ages, joined the VVS in his teens and attained the rank of general by the time he was 30. During the GP War Savitsky had flown the I-16, LaGG-3, La-5, Yak-1 and Spitfire, accruing a tally of at least 22 personal and 3 group kills by the end of the conflict. A double HSU, 'Ye Ya' flew some 216 combat sorties over the Far East, Moscow, Kuban Peninsula and Berlin. That the La-5F was still an effective fighter right up to the last year of the war was proven by Maj P S Kutakhov of 19 Gv.IAP, who scored many of his 14 individual and 28 shared victories in the type over the Karlian Front in 1944/45.

La-7

Basically an aerodynamically refined version of the La-5, the La-7 was first flight tested in late 1943 and then issued for service trials early the following year. By May 1944 it had started to equip VVS fighter regiments, where its top speed of 423 mph, improved climbing performance and

53

greater range made it the favoured mount amongst leading Soviet aces and Guards regiments alike. The fiercely independent Maj Sultan Amet-Khan (a former Hurricane ace who would eventually finish the war with 30 individual and 19 shared kills) used the fighter to great effect, as did Ivan Kozhedub, who shot down his last kill of the war – the Me 262A of 1./KG(J) 54's Unteroffizier Kurt Lange – over Frankfurt-am-Oder whilst flying a La-7.

A factory-fresh La-7 is seen on display in Moscow in early 1945

Ivan Kozhedub flew La-7 'White 27' during his time as Deputy CO of 176.Gv.IAP in early 1945. Seen on display in the late 1960s, the aircraft wears the triple Gold Stars of the HSU and his full tally of 62 kills

An unidentified La-7 is seen on its final approach to land

MiG-3

As the first fighter to successfully reach frontline service from the now famous Mikoyan-Gurevich design bureau, the MiG-3 was a very demanding machine to fly well in peacetime, let alone in combat. One of those pilots who was thrust into war strapped into a MiG-3 was Aleksandr Pokryshkin, who succinctly described the fighter in the following quote;

'I liked it at once. It could be compared with a frisky, fiery, horse – in experienced hands it was to run like an arrow, but if you lost control you finished up beneath its hooves.'

Pokryshkin's mount on 22 June 1941 was one of the 1289 examples of the type which had already been delivered to the VVS by the time of the invasion. Indeed, it was the most prolific of the three new generation fighters at the outbreak of war, and from forming just 10 per cent of the frontline force in mid-1941, this figure had risen to 41.2 per cent by year end.

Essentially a hastily improved MiG-1, the MiG-3 had been the result of design work carried out by former Polikarpov design team members Artem I Mikoyan and Mikhail Y Gurevich at the OKB (Experimental Design Bureau). Whilst Mikoyan and Gurevich were the chief designers, other specialists involved on the project included designers Brunov, Andriyanov and Seletsky, as well as the aerodynamicist Matyuk. Following a January 1939 meeting at the Kremlin (again presided over by Stalin) in which new specifications for fighter aircraft were issued, a new OKB was formed to be headed by A I Mikoyan in GAZ No 1 at Vnukovo aerodrome in Moscow.

Initially designated the I-200, prototypes of the MiG-1 were flown by a fleet of test pilots including A N Yekatov, S P Suprun, P M Stefanovsky and A G Kochetkov – although the former was killed following an engine failure in one of the early MiGs, the remaining test pilots survived the somewhat fraught testing of the MiG-1 to join their colleagues at the Scientific and Research Institute of the Air Force

MiG-3 pilots applaud a speech on combat tactics given by Aleksandr Pokryshkin, whilst in the background one of their number prepares to go off and put the ace's teachings to the test against the Luftwaffe

(NII VVS) within the MiG-3-equipped 401. and 402. IAPs. Indeed, Stefan Suprun and Pyotr Stefanovsky would eventually become commanding officers of these regiments, which were directly subordinated to the Soviet Supreme Command (VGK) – Suprun was soon shot down near Tolochino, by Vitebsk, and was replaced as CO by K K Kokkinaki. From 30 June to the end of October 1941, 401.IAP claimed some 54 enemy aircraft shot down with the MiG-3, after which the regiment was disbanded.

The first MiG-3 victory of the GP War was a Dornier Do 215 claimed by Lt D Kokorev on the opening morning of *Barbarossa*, followed shortly after by a Henschel Hs 126 observation aircraft which fell to the guns of Lt Mironov. Later that same day MiG-3 pilot Capt Karmanov claimed three kills over Kishinyev, in Moldavia – all three pilots hailed from the short-lived 401.IAP.

Pyotr Stefanovsky's 402.IAP lasted far longer than Suprun's regiment. In the thick of fighting from early July, initial successes fell to Capt Afanasi Grigor'yevich Proshkov, who shot down a Do 215 in Veliki Luki, and Lt M S Chenosov, who claimed the destruction of a Bf 110 over Nevel.

In mid-July Stepanovsky was withdrawn from 402.IAP and appointed to command the fighter component of the air defence of the Western Sector of Moscow, which consisted of ten fighter regiments – two of these were based at Tushino aerodrome with MiG-3 fighters. Many legendary VVS pilots 'cut their teeth' in this fighter component, including future NII test pilot Mark Gallai, who would later fly the first Me 262 to fall into Soviet hands.

During the defence of Moscow the MiG-3 was also used as a night-fighter. Although no longer led by Stefanovsky, 402.IAP continued to play a significant role in fighter combat both by day and night, and by early August the regiment had been attached to 57.Composite Air Division. As part of this force it took part in operations over Stara Russa and Novgorod, before participating the action over the North-Western Front during the hostile winter of 1941/42. The final days of the MiG-3 era found 402.IAP attacking the enemy bridgehead in the Taman peninsula in early 1942.

With their war-weary mount now beginning to show serious signs of obsolescence in the face of new Luftwaffe fighters, the regiment relinquished their MiG-3s in the late spring of 1942 and re-equipped with other types. 402.IAP would go on to fight over Magnushev, Stargard and Pila, before finishing the war flying patrols over Berlin with Yak-9s – by which point its pilots had claimed over 800 victories.

It turned out that the somewhat ubiquitous MiG-3 could operate in any of the climatic extremes found in the USSR, from the temperate steppes of south-western Ukraine to the polar 'wasteland' surrounding the strategic port of Murmansk. Although MiG-3s had been finally withdrawn from frontline units by early 1944, the type remained in service until the end of the war with Defence (PVO) fighter regiments.

An aircraft with both capability and vices, the MiG-3 provoked the following comment from Aleksandr Pokryshkin;

'Its designers rarely succeeded in matching both the fighter's flight characteristics with its firepower . . . the operational advantages of the

The distinctive shape of a quartet of MiG-3s lined up at dusk. Many VVS fighters were lost in the opening bombing raids of *Barbarossa* because regiments were caught with their aircraft parked in this 'parade ground' fashion

MiG-3 seemed to be overshadowed by its certain defects. However, these advantages could undoubtedly be exploited by a pilot who was able to find them.'

Yak-3

Developed from the critically important Yak-1, A S Yakovlev's Yak-3 made its debut in frontline service over Kursk just as the former type was being phased out of production following the delivery of the 8721st aircraft. Building on the success of the Yak-1, the -3 would achieve huge popularity amongst Soviet pilots due to its crisp handling, impressive manoeuvrability, high top speed (407 mph at 10,170 ft) and potent armament.

As described earlier in this volume, the Yak-3 was employed to deadly effect by the *Normandie-Niemen Groupe*, whilst Soviet pilots of the calibre of double HSU recipient Maj S D Lugansky (who gained most of his 37 personal and 6 group victories with the Yak-3 over Stalingrad and then Ukrainian Fronts) and third-ranking ace Pokryshkin also enjoyed successful spells with the Yakovlev fighter.

As with the La-5, the Yak-3 enabled Soviet pilots to feel confident even in combat against superior numbers, as was graphically demonstrated on 17 July 1944 when a group of just eight Yak-3s flew headlong into a formation of sixty enemy aircraft, including its fighter escort. In the subsequent melee, the Luftwaffe lost three Ju 87s and four Bf 109Gs without reply.

The total production of the Yak-3 numbered some 4848 aircraft by the time the last one left the factory in early 1946.

This official Ministry of Information photograph depicts Yak-7Bs of 3.IAK, sporting their winged-star emblems, during the early days of the Battle of the Kuban River in April 1943. The original caption attached to the back of the print reads, 'A long row of warplanes – Gift of the Collective Farmers of the Autonomous Soviet Socialist Republic of Bashkirian to the Red Air Force'

Another official Ministry of Information photograph, this time showing a Yak-1 being serviced behind a group of Red Army soldiers enjoying a break from the fighting in 1943. The orriginal caption reads, 'A Soviet fighter group operating in the Mozdok area has to its credit the destruction of several river crossings and large quantities of enemy men during a seven day offensive. In this time the group also shot down seven enemy aircraft. Picture shows – Guns under repair at dispersal point'

Yak-9

Introduced to VVS operations in late 1943, the Yak-9 served as both a frontline fighter and fighter-bomber. With the latter role firmly in mind, Yakovlev designers installed large calibre guns to enable the aircraft to undertake anti-armour, anti-shipping and anti-bomber roles. Designated the Yak-9T (T for 'tyazhely', or 'heavy') series, these variants included air-

craft fitted with 23, 37 and 45 mm cannon firing anti-tank projectiles. The more standard Yak-9 was favourably compared by it pilots with both the Bf 109G and the recently arrived Fw 190A-3/A-4 in performance terms. The total production for all Yak-9 variants was around the 16,700 mark, and by mid-1944 this prolifically-constructed aircraft outnumbered the combined total figure of all other Soviet fighters then serving in frontline VVS regiments!

Top Yak aces included Ivan I Kleschchev who, having initially fought in the Khalkin-Gol conflict, was awarded a HSU in May 1942 whilst serving as CO of 521.IAP on the Kalinin front – he scored gained 6 personal and 13 group kills during this time. The following month he was posted to command the newly-formed 434.IAP firstly in Moscow, and then to the west of Stalingrad, where he again saw action in the Yak-1. These were eventually replaced by Yak-7s and then Yak-9s, Kleschchev using these fighters to raise his score to 16 individual and 32 group kills before he was shot down and injured.

Lt L K Vastolkin of 8.IAP, VVS, ChF, waves to the camera prior to taking-off on a combat sortie in his Yak-1. This regiment operated in the Sevastopl area during the spring of 1942

This brightly marked Yak-9, with pilot V T Gugridze in the cockpit, was photographed during the summer of 1944 in Byelorussia. The inscription translates to 'For Brother Shota', whilst the faint writing on the arrow says 'To the West'

Forced landings were commonplace near to the frontline, as pilots found that they could not coax their damaged aircraft back home. This Yak-9 has been put down rather too close for comfort for the residents of the farmhouse in the background. Such an event almost always invited considerable attention from the local populace when the aircraft came down in a residential area

Another high-scoring Yakovlev pilot was M D Baranov, who had achieved at least 24 victories with his Yak-1 before he was killed in a flying accident on 17 January 1943. Towards the end of the war Yak-9 pilot L I Sivko of 812.IAP shot down the first Me 262 to fall victim to the VVS on 22 March 1945. He was then in turn targeted by a second Messerschmitt jet fighter and swiftly shot down and killed – possibly by Franz Schall, one of the leading Me 262 jet aces of the war (see *Aircraft of the Aces 17 Lufwaffe Jet Aces of World War 2* for more details).

STALIN'S INFLUENCE

Joseph Stalin, as supreme Commander in Chief of the Red Army, oversaw, and to a large extent controlled, the activities of the Stavka (the Supreme Headquarters). He was keenly interested in the conduct of aerial war, and would actively involve himself with senior air force commanders and aircraft designers. For such individuals, Stalin's personal involvement was both intimidating and inhibiting, for all knew of his ruthless and murderous potential, which had been amply demonstrated during the purges of the late 1930s.

Leading fighter aircraft designer Aleksandr Yakovlev felt the force of Stalin's informed interest and, indeed, judgment during a meeting in the latter's office near to the Stavka, within the walls of the Kremlin. He recalled in his postwar memoirs being summoned along with P V Dement'yev, who was then in charge of aviation production, to Stalin's office. Upon their entry into the latter's 'inner sanctum', they were confronted by a piece of cracked Yak-9 wing fabric draped on the table in the office. Following a quietly ominous beginning, Stalin pointed to the fabric and asked them whether they had any knowledge of the problem that had afflicted it. Before they could answer, he read to them a field report which stated that the wing coverings of the Yak-9 were peeling off due to the stress of combat.

Yakovlev and Dement'yev duly acknowledged that they were aware of the problem, which had arisen because of the employment of inferior glues and dyes in production plants, and that they were presently attempting to find solutions. Stalin fired still more questions, receiving increasingly anxious replies until he finally exploded and accused them of providing support for Hitler by producing aircraft that would break up in operational circumstances. Yakovlev and Dement'yev were mortified by this verbal attack, and genuinely concerned for their physical well-being. Dement'yev promised Stalin that he would correct the problem within two weeks, and luckily for them both he managed to do just that!

LEND-LEASE AEROPLANES

Aside from the multifarious fighter types of Soviet origin employed by the VVS during the GP War, aircraft from the United States and Great

Britain were also supplied in large quantities to the USSR chiefly under lend-lease arrangements. Some 9438 fighters were supplied from the USA mainly via the Alaskan-Siberian Ferry route, the most prolific of these being the Bell P-39 Airacobra, which was flown with great flair and success by Pokryshkin and Rechkalov.

Indeed, fighters formed the largest proportion of all aircraft types delivered to the USSR, accounting for around 72 per cent of all military types supplied. The principal British types were the Spitfire (mostly MK VBs) and the Hurricane, the latter being the first lend-lease aircraft of them all to arrive in the Soviet Union – some 2952 Hawker fighters were eventually despatched to the USSR. The following short account explores the initial activity which surrounded the delivery of the first ex-RAF Hurricanes in the autumn of 1941.

One of the pilots sent to the Soviet Union to help with the transfer of aircraft to the VVS was Eric 'Ginger' Carter, who was then serving as a Hurricane pilot No 81 Sqn. His unit had been seconded to the hastily-formed No 151 Wing, which was based at Vayenga, near Murmansk, upon its arrival in the USSR. He recalled;

'Some 39 of us were sent out by Churchill two weeks after they (the USSR) had "come in on our side". We went out on a luxury liner *Llanstephen Castle*, which had been converted for use as a troop carrier.

No less than 4924 Bell P-39 Airacobras reached the USSR during the GP War, these aircraft travelling by one of four routes: ALSIB (i.e. the Alaskan-Siberian Ferry Route); by sea direct from the USA to Murmansk; re-directed by sea from the UK; or by sea to the Persian Gulf (Iran), and then onto the USSR. This P-39 served with Guards regiment 21 Gv.IAP, and the inscription indicates that it was donated by the Kolkhoze workers of Krasnoyarsh. Standing in front of the aircraft are regiment pilots V N Yakimov (right) and N I Proshenkov (left)

We assembled as Archangel and were sent up to defend Murmansk, at the entrance to the White Sea. Had the Germans been able to isolate this strategic port, no outside help would have reached Russia from the UK.'

Whilst the majority of No 151 Wing left for Murmansk, some 170 miles north of the line of latitude that marks the Arctic Circle, a small team remained in Archangel (some 300 miles south of Murmansk) tasked with assembling the 15 crated Hurricanes which had trav-

As the 15 kill markings on this P-39 indicate, Snr Lt O V Zyuzin of 11.Gv.IAP, VVS, ChF, was indeed a triple ace. He received the HSU as a result of his successes on 16 May 1944

elled over on the *Llanstephen Castle*. It was at this point that a close liaison between the RAF and Soviet personnel first commenced, for the former quickly discovered that assembly tool kits had not been provided for the crated Hurricanes – of particular concern were the missing airscrew spanners.

Contact was made with Maj-Gen A A Kuznetsov, Commander of the Northern Fleet Air Force, and he duly ordered that a team of Soviet technicians be tasked with con-

structing improvised tools, many of which were made overnight from drawings on envelopes. The men further collaborated with the RAF team in the actual assembly of the Hurricanes themselves, all of which were made ready to fly in only nine days. Further problems were then encountered with the aircraft's armament, as it was found that the Browning guns delivered to Archangel from Murmansk on 9 September 1941 aboard two Soviet destroyers lacked both rear sear release units and fire and safe units – they were also fitted with Mk I blast tube adaptors, which were unsuitable for fitment into the Hurricane IIBs operated by No 151 Wing. Through a combination of Soviet improvisation and British ingenuity, the groundcrews eventually got all the Hurricanes serviceable, and the wing wasted no time in going into action, as Eric 'Ginger' Carter recounts;

'We found that we were mainly involved in escort duties, and were there to teach the Russian pilots how to fly the Hurricane. We made contact with the enemy (the Finnish Air Force) on many occasions, for they were only ten miles away. By the time we had got our wheels up and flaps and pitch correct, we were in their circuit, and so there were quite a lot of skirmishes. Due to our close proximity they would bomb us quite often. In fact during one raid one of our chaps managed to take-off straight from the dispersal point!

'The problem for this chap was that to test his magnetos he had to run his engine up to full revs. Normally, the procedure was to put two groundcrew on the tail to prevent it coming up under full power.

'Although there were bombs falling all around, the two lads thought that the pilot was simply testing his mags, whereas he was trying to get into the air as quickly as he could. The Hurricane took off with the two men on the tail, got to about 500 ft and then spun in. The two groundcrew were killed instantly and the pilot died later from his injuries after returning to England.

Proudly wearing the Gold Star of the HSU, Maj V F Sirotin of 17.IAP is seen sat in the cockpit of his P-39 in early 1945. Twenty-one kills adorn the cockpit door of his Airacobra, forward of which is an impressive personal emblem depicting an eagle chasing a German aircraft away from a ship – it is likely that Sirotin was involved in convoy protection in the Baltic region

16.Gv.IAP pilots flock around their commander, Aleksandr Pokryshkin, soon after his return from yet another successful sortie. It is possible that this photo was taken during July/August 1944 when Pokryshkin learned that he was to receive the HSU for the third time, thus becoming the first VVS pilot to receive this accolade

26.Gv.IAP, PVO, was equipped with Spitfire Mk IX fighters for defensive duties of Leningrad towards the end of the war. By May 1945 some 964 Mk IXs had been issued to the VVS, supplanting the batch of 143 Mk Vs passed to the Soviets in March 1943

'We primarily engaged Bf 109s during our time in Russia, and we tended to fly in pairs when on escort duties in order to protect the tail of the leader. We shot down 16 enemy aircraft and were paid £240 for this feat by Stalin, which was of course a lot of money in those days – it could have bought two detached houses back then! The CO, Isherwood (Wg Cdr H N G Ramsbottom-Isherwood), wouldn't let us have it, passing it on instead to the RAF Benevolent Fund, as he reasoned we would be shooting each other down in order to get the bounty!

'It would be fair to say that we shot down a lot more than the 16 enemy aircraft both Nos 81 and 134 Sqns were credited with. It was the case that Russian anti-aircraft batteries would put in claims even though they might have been way off course with their shooting. We were instructed not to pursue a claim so that we did not compete with our Russian colleagues, and thus did not offend Stalin, who was, in any case, not keen to publicise our involvement. This was not the case with the Russian pilots who we taught to fly the Hurricane. We seemed to get on well together – we had to!'

Carter found that the language problems were not a great impediment to teaching the young Russian pilots to fly the Hurricane;

'Although we had two interpreters, a pilot is generally able to communicate what he is trying to do in any language, and the Russians seemed to cotton-on quickly to our instructions.'

In practice, whilst both Nos 81 and 134 Sqns escorted Russian bombers on many of the missions undertaken during the early autumn months of 1941, the main task of training VVS pilots designated to fly the Hurricane fell to the latter unit – therefore, the lion's share of the combat claims made by RAF pilots during this period were filed by No 81 Sqn pilots.

VVS Hurricanes

The 72nd Regiment of the Russian Naval Air Fleet, Northern Fleet Air Force (72.IAP VVS, SF), was one of the units in northern Russia which fell under the command of Maj-Gen A A Kuznetsov, Commander of the Northern Fleet Air Force. The 72nd Regiment was picked out as the first unit to be trained to fly the British fighter, and Kuznetsov played an important role in ensuring that the RAF were treated with respect and diplomacy, which duly set the tone for the collaboration between the his personnel and the RAF.

The first VVS pilot to be introduced to the RAF contingent was an instructor by the name of Raputsokov, who held the rank of captain. Sadly, he failed to make a single flight in the Hurricane for he was killed with his crew when the Soviet bomber he was piloting crashed near the RAF base at Vayenga following an operational sortie. Two further pilots, Kuharienko and Safonov, were posted to liaise with No 151 Wing, and they were duly amongst the first trio of Russian pilots to fly the Hurricane. Capt Kuharienko, who formed a close friendship with Flt Lt Jack Ross, DFC, appears to have had a reputation for being a lively character, and in his first flight he took off with minimum preparation, erratically taxying with the rudder bias in the incorrect position, before struggling into the air and proceeding to beat-up the airfield of Vayenga, before safely landing.

The second pilot to take-off in a Hurricane, 26-year-old Boris Froktistorich Safonov, was already a successful I-16 ace by the time he arrived in Archangel. Initially he made no mistakes as he took off and performed

This Ministry of Information photograph, taken in October 1941, shows the diminutive figure of Flt Lt Jack Ross of No 134 Sqn unbuckling his parachute under the amused gaze of a Soviet soldier. Ross, who had served with No 17 Sqn throughout the Battle of Britain, had scored 2 and 3 shared destroyed and 2 probables (none woth No 151 Wing, however) by the time he was lost whilst on a patrol over the Irish Sea on 6 January 1942. His Hurricane IIB had suffered engine failure during a routine flight from Eglinton, in Northern Ireland, and although he successfully ditched the stricken fighter, Ross was never seen again

Right
The Ministry of Information caption for this photo reads, 'Shoulder to Shoulder: British Air Technician Freeman trains Soviet pilot V Maksimovich to fly a Hurricane'

Middle
Boris Safonov (extreme right) and three 72.IAP pilots engage in animated conversation with pilot Flt Lt 'Mickey' Rook. The latter pilot had served with No 504 Sqn from 1938 until one of its flights was used as the nucleus around which No 134 Sqn was created in July 1941. Rook survived the war with a score of 2 and 1 shared destroyed and 1 probable – the shared destroyed was claimed during his time with No 151 Wing in the USSR (*Petrov*)

Below
A VVS pilot prepares to climb into the cockpit of an idling Hurricane IIB. The installation of Soviet armament (two ShVAK 20 mm cannon and a pair of Beresin VB 12.7 mm machine guns) in place of the British weaponry was one of the first modifications made by the VVS following their receipt of the Hurricanes from No 151 Wing

A group of VVS pilots receive 'words of wisdom' from an instructor whilst sat beneath the wing of a Hurricane IIB in 1942 – in the background can be seen an I-16. Regiments within the Northern Fleet Air Force would often be concurrently equipped with two or more operational types, and 2.Gv.IAP, commanded by Boris Safonov in the spring of 1942, had I-16s, Hurricanes and P-40 Tomahawks on strength all at the same time! An additional, feature of VVS operations throughout the GP War was the extent to which they constructed decoy airfields and aeroplanes to distract Luftwaffe bombing attacks away from their 'real' bases. The Soviet Union was probably more skilled than any other country in this respect during the war

three circuit and bumps prior to landing. However, on the point of his final recovery Safonov ran through a large puddle – perhaps more appropriately described as a lake, as the aerodrome had been waterlogged following heavy rain – and damaged the aircraft's flaps. Despite incurring the displeasure of the watching Maj-Gen Kuznetsov, Safonov went on to become a brilliant leader, and was the first ace of the GP War to receive a high public profile.

This latter point is reinforced by the fact that Safonov appears in many of the photographs which exist some 56 years after the event. Aside from being something of a self-publicist, it was also discovered that he was a brilliant shot with a revolver, a fact that came to light during impromptu revolver competitions held between the Soviets and the RAF.

Prior to Safonov completing his brief flight, Kuznetsov himself had become the first VVS pilot to fly one of No 151 Wing's Hurricanes, a feat which took place on 25 September 1941 – his interpreter throughout the

This very Hurricane IIB (Z5252) was the aircraft in which Maj-Gen A A Kuznetsov, Commander of the Northern Fleet Air Force, became the first Soviet pilot to fly the Hawker fighter on 25 September, 1941. Following his brief sortie, Kuznetsov was presented with the aircraft by No 151 Wing, which had decorated the Hurricane with the major-general's own number, '01', as well as full VVS red star markings

This photograph shows ex-VVS personnel from 72.IAP who were guests of honour at a reunion of No 151 Wing pilots and groundcrews held in the Midlands town of Rugby in 1995. Included in this shot is at least one HSU recipient, who unfortunately remains anonymous! The reunion was organised by Peter Fearn, the current Managing Director of Broquet International – the latter was founded by the late Henry Broquet who, as a 26-year-old RAF technician in the autumn of 1941, had been sent to the USSR to work with Soviet scientists, the RAF and VVS in an effort to find a way to improve the dreadfully poor fuel octane rating which was threatening to cut short the Hurricane's operational life in-theatre. The fuel catalyst that was eventually produced was patented by Broquet after the war, and is still marketed today (*Peter Fearn*)

RAF's stay was an ex-school mistress, who wrote down the cockpit drill for him. Immediately after completing the flight Kuznetsov was presented with an aircraft (ex-No 81 Sqn aircraft Z5252), complete with his personal number '01' and full Red Star markings. He remained as Commander of the Northern Fleet Air Force until December 1942, and subsequently became a HSU on 6 December 1949.

Following these first flights, four Soviet pilots – Kuharienko, Safonov, Yacobenko and Andrushin – were given pivotal tasks in instructing other VVS pilots converting onto the Hurricane. Yacobenko was subsequently given command of one of first VVS Hurricane squadrons, but he lost his life in a night attack on the German airfield at Petsamo soon after. The RAF contingent received this news shortly before they commenced their long journey home to the UK.

Future VVS Hurricane aces included Sultan Amet-Khan, who achieved his first kill (a Ju 88) with the Hawker fighter whilst flying with 4.IAP over Yaroslavl. A two-time HSU, Amet-Khan was to lose his life in a flying accident in 1971 whilst serving as a NII VVS test pilot.

THE LEADING ACES

Postwar lists of Soviet fighter aces of the GP War have all shared one over-riding characteristic – there is *no* standard list (see the appendices for comparative listings). This is the direct result of conflicting 'evidence' held within Russian records, which has made it extremely difficult for anyone to produce a definitive list of the leading Soviet fighter aces.

Some of the worst 'sources' of them all for inflated kill claims are the myriad biographies ostensibly produced both during and after the war by Soviet aces. Invariably written in heroic prose by party 'ghost writers', these works were rich in rhetoric about the fascist enemy and ever faithful to the Stalinist system, but were usually very short on documented fact. Many of the leading VVS RKKA aces published their memoirs in postwar years, but most of these volumes have never been translated into the English language.

Current Soviet aviation journals like *Aeroplan*, *Aviatsiya/Kosmonavtika* and *Krylya Rodiny* do occasionally contain biographies, interviews and lists of aces of the Soviet Air Force, some of which have been painstakingly researched. In the United Kingdom, one of the most comprehensive collections of these biographies, autobiographies and retrospective academic studies outside the Soviet Union is held by the Russian Aviation Research Trust.

Within the Soviet Union itself, recent opportunities for aviation historians to access VVS records – a seemingly impossible research avenue not so many years ago – may complicate rather than clarify the situation. For example, Finnish aviation historians have recently discovered an even

An early free scoring fighter pilot was Snr Lt Mikhail J Vasiliev of 4.Gv.IAP, VVS, KBF, who had downed some 22 enemy aircraft by the time he killed in action on 5 May 1942. Here, Vasiliev had just landed his I-16 *Tip 17* 'White 28' after completing a sortie over the frontline. The ace was posthumously awarded the HSU on 14 June 1942

This page
Maj Aleksei Alelyukhin poses with his La-7, which carries the inscription 'To Alelyukhin from the collective of factory No 41 of the People's Commissariate of Aviation Industry'. His impressive tally of 40 personal kills and 17 shared was accumulated during the 600 operational sorties that he completed – Alelyukhin met the enemy on no less than 258 occasions. As a captain with 9.Gv.IAP, he was awarded the Gold Star of the HSU twice in 1943, on 24 August and 1 November (*Petrov*)

greater disparity between admitted Soviet loss rates and proven Finnish Air Force claims during the latter part of the Continuation War than had previously been anticipated. So it can be concluded that no definitive history is ever likely to be produced on VVS aces simply because of the unreliability of the available source material.

Bearing this in mind, the following pages aim to provide a 'window' through which the careers of several of the 'leading lights' within the VVS can be viewed, without wishing to present conclusive evidence of their place in the 'pecking order' of Soviet fighter aces.

VVS Aces 1936-40

Between 1936 and 1940 the USSR was involved in eight conflicts, with major participation by the VVS occurring in the Spanish Civil War, China and the Khalkin-Gol conflicts against the Japanese, and the first of two bitter wars over Finnish territory throughout the winter of 1939/40.

Aside from being the first real test of Soviet men, machinery and tactics, the Spanish Civil War was also the longest conflict in which VVS fighter pilots were involved prior to *Barbarossa*. Spain was to become the proving ground for many of the future aces of the GP War, with the most successful of these being P V Rychagov with a score believed to be around the 15-kill mark. He was later promoted and transferred to China, although he failed to add to his score in the Far East and was subsequently executed in Stalin's purges. I A Layeyev claimed 12 personal kills in Spain, followed by another 2 over Khalkin-Gol, and another Civil War ace, S P Danliov, also went on to achieve further victories over Mongolia.

Undoubtedly the most successful VVS pilot of this period was S I Gritsevets, who became the first Soviet airman to receive the HSU on two occasions. These awards reflected his status as the top scoring Soviet

Vladimir I Popkov received his first Gold Star of the HSU on 8 September 1943 whilst serving as a senior lieutenant, and his second award some six weeks after the end of the war as a captain. Popkov stands, somewhat bashfully, next to his La-5, which sports 33 kills markings, someof which are rather faint! Popkov served exclusively with 5.Gv.IAP, flying 325 sorties and claiming 41 personal kills from 107 operational engagements with the Luftwaffe (*Petrov*)

fighter pilot of Khalkin-Gol with 12 individual enemy kills. Earlier, he had flown the I-16 *Rata* in Spain as the squadron commander of 70.IAP, prior to the unit becoming one of the first in the VVS to convert onto the I-153 in Khalkin-Gol. The Soviet propaganda machine duly made Gritsevets a national hero in the USSR, stating that his combined tally from Spain and Khalkin-Gol was no less than 42 individual and group kills.

After completing his second operational tour, Gritsevets was posted back to the USSR on 15 September 1939 and sent to 66.IAB (Fighter Aviation Brigade, which preceded the implementation of regiments – 66.IAB was made up of 33. and 41. IAPs), which was due to operate in support of the invasion of East Poland. Landing at his new aerodrome in Byelorussia, Gritsevets' aircraft was hit by another machine and he was killed in the collision.

Other fighter aces in Mongolia included Zherdiyev, who accumulated 11 personal victories, whilst a further 9 Soviet pilots filed claims for between 6 and 9 individual kills apiece. Some pilots could boast bigger scores than these, but the greater percentage were group claims. For example, F V Vasil'yev had 30 kills, but only 7 were credited as personal claims, whilst A V Vorozheykin gained 20 kills, 13 of which were group victories. As a sign of the overall success enjoyed by the VVS during the Khalkin-Gol conflict, the HSU was awarded on 26 occasions.

Another readily identifiable fighter ace of the pre-*Barborossa* era was G P Kravchenko, who went on to achieve combat success, high rank and a fine reputation as a powerful tactician of airpower prior to his death in 1943. His operational career began in China in 1936, and on his very first mission he was injured when making an attack on three Japanese bombers. Managing to carry through the attack, Kravchenko shot down all three enemy aircraft before nursing his I-16 back to base. He was subsequently credited with one personal claim and two group kills. The former victory was the first of Kravchenko's nine personal claims for the destruction of enemy aircraft in China as confirmed by Soviet authorities. By February 1939 he had been made a HSU, and he was soon promoted to command 22.IAP in the fighting over Khalkin-Gol during 1939. A second HSU followed in November 1939, and the following year he was promoted to general.

Left and below
These photos show the La-5s of 159.IAP, this regiment being involved in the defence of Leningrad in mid-1944. The period Russian caption attached to the photo at left says, 'Two aces P Likholetov and V Zotov defending Leningrad destroyed 47 fascist aircraft'. The latter was credited with 28 personal and 10 group kills, and both pilots were awarded the HSU
(*St Petersburg State Archives of Photo, Phono and Cinematographic Records*)

FINLAND

Unlike VVS operations in China and Mongolia, or the 'volunteer' force which had fought in Spain, the first of the two air wars against Finland produced no individual Soviet fighter aces. Despite outlandishly high claims (VVS pilots were credited with 381 Finnish aircraft destroyed), only three Soviet fighter pilots claimed four kills – A F Semyonov, M Sokolov and V M Naydenko.

Despite an overwhelming numerical superiority of at least 10-to-1, the VVS RKKA was unable to translate this advantage into success in the air. Even the implementation of the lessons learned in Spain and China failed to secure air superiority for the VVS over the snow-covered Finnish landscape.

VVS pilots equipped with Soviet fighters designed in the 1930s were simply no match for the cosmopolitan Finnish force made up of equally ancient aircraft, but flown by highly trained and competitive Finnish combat pilots. The latter made great use of their motley fleet of Fokker D XXIs, Gloster Gladiators and Fiat G.50s, which easily measured up to the I-16s and I-153s of the VVS in combat. In recent years the Soviet authorities have admitted losses of 579 of their own aircraft, compared with a figure of just 68 for the Finns!

Far left
P Ya Likholetov claimed 25 personal and 5 group kills during the GP War
(*St Petersburg State Archives of Photo, Phono and Cinematographic Records*)

THE GREAT PATRIOTIC WAR

Historians have generally agreed that Ivan Nikolaevich Kozhedub, with a tally of 62 personal victories, was the highest scoring fighter pilot of the Red Air Force during the GP War. Indeed, Kozhedub's score also makes him the uncontested 'ace of aces' amongst all Allied fighter pilots of World War 2.

Kozhedub was not alone in scoring 50 or more personal kills, some six other pilots (Grigori Rechkalov, Aleksandr Pokryshkin, Nikolai Gulayev, Kirill Yevstigneyev, Nikolai Skomorokhov, possibly Nikolai Shutt, according to at least one Soviet historian, and Boris Glinka), achieving higher scores than the leading ace of the Western Allies, Sqn Ldr M T StJ Pattle, with an unsubstantiated tally of 50+ kills.

Petr Pokryshev, seen here standing at the extreme left, flew Yak-7s with 159.IAP. His aircraft was one of a number of wartime machines flown by notable pilots to be subsequently displayed postwar – Pokryshev's fighter became part of the Museum of Defence collection in Leningrad. Its placement within this exhibit was most apt as its pilot had been made a HSU on 10 February 1943 whilst flying as a captain with 154.IAP in defence of the beleaguered city. Pokryshev gained his second Gold Star whilst commanding 159.IAP, and his final kill tally is estimated to have been between 22 and 38 personal victories, plus several accredited group claims (*Petrov*)

Aircraft designer meets fighter ace – the designer of the La-5, Semyon A Lavochkin (right) stands with La-5FN ace Col V F Golubev (centre), CO of 4.Gv.IAP, VVS, KBF, in 1945, and a second highly decorated, but anonymous, pilot. Golubev received the Gold Star of the HSU on 23 October 1942, and finished the war with 39 personal kills (*Petrov*)

IVAN NIKOLAEVICH KOZHEDUB

Examining I N Kozhedub's career in closer detail, he flew some 326 operational sorties during the war, engaging the enemy on 126 occasions – all of his victories were against piston-engined aircraft, with the exception of one Me 262. Kozhedub flew the La-5FN and the La-7 with great success, and his exploits were widely reported to an adoring Soviet public, who got to know his face through huge posters that were displayed in public areas extolling the populace to 'Fight like Kozhedub'. As a communist party member, Kozhedub was the ideal role model for aspiring young Soviet fighter pilots to follow.

During the GP War, he was awarded the HSU on two occasions, and a third award was made shortly after the war had ended. At the time of the first award on 14 February 1944, Kozhedub was a senior lieutenant and squadron leader with 240.IAP. Just six months later he received the second HSU, by which time he had become been promoted to captain and made deputy commander of 176.Gv.IAP. On 19 August 1945, he received his final award as a major, and still deputy commander of the 176. Gv.IAP.

This staged postwar photo shows triple Gold Star winners Kozhedub and Pokryshkin who, between them, destroyed 121 Luftwaffe aircraft in combat. Although very different personalities, both pilots were supreme combat fighters, and both went on to to enjoy successful military careers in the 'Cold War' air force, eventually attaining the rank of air marshals

Kozhedub commenced flying jet-powered fighters in 1948, and by April 1951 he was undertaking operational sorties in MiG-15 fighters over Korea. He went on to become a Colonel-General of Aviation in 1974 and was promoted to air marshal on 7 August 1985 – ten years earlier, Kozhedub's politically fervent memoirs *Vernost'otchizne* (*Faithfulness to the Fatherland*) had been published in Russia. Air Marshal Ivan Kozhedub finally died in August 1991 aged 71.

GRIGORI RECHKALOV

Just behind Kozhedub in the list of Soviet aces is Grigori Rechkalov, an outstanding fighter pilot who ran into significant personal conflict with his divisional commander, Aleksandr Pokryshkin. Like Kozhedub, Grigori Andreevich Rechkalov had come into operational flying comparatively late in the war, yet managed to build-up an enormous score.

He had begun his operational career with 216.IAD of the 4.VA on the North Caucasian Front during the Battle over the Kuban in the early summer of 1943, before being transferred to 9.IAD over the 2nd Ukrainian Front. During this time Rechkalov had occasionally flown as wingman to 16.Gv.IAP ace A I Pokryshkin, although as the war moved into its final year these opportunities became less frequent as the latter's duties as divisional commander kept him more on the ground than in the air. Accusations have persisted since the end of the war that Rechkalov was more concerned with building his own score than protecting the operational interests of the squadron as a whole. There seems to have been some substance to this allegation, his critics citing an episode in May 1944

The pilot seen posing second from the left in this group photo is Grigori Rechkalov, the second highest scoring Allied ace of World War 2 – his P-39 serves as a suitable backdrop to the shot. Rechkalov flew with Pokryshkin's 16.Gv.IAP, and despite a chequered history in terms of his relationships with senior officers, he proved to be an outstanding combat pilot. He scored 56 personal victories and a further 5 shared during the course of 609 sorties, engaging the enemy on 122 occasions. He was awarded the Gold Star of the HSU on two occasions, the first on 24 May 1943 and the second on 1 July 1944 (*Petrov*)

when Rechkalov was commander of 16.Gv.IAP. With his regiment in action over Prut, he was reported for having failed to provide his pilots with leadership, being more interested in pursuing his personal battle with the Luftwaffe instead. Upon the unit's return to base, it was discovered that three of Rechkalov's pilots had been shot down, and a furious Pokryshkin went directly to the corps commander, Gen Utin, to lodge an official complaint. Having secured the latter's backing, Pokryshkin then dismissed Rechkalov from his post as CO of 16.Gv.IAP, replacing him with another well-known ace, Boris Glinka.

Despite his apparent failings as a leader, Grigori Rechkalov was nevertheless both a superb aerial shot and an extremely skilled pilot of the P-39Q Airacobra, and by war's end his total had reached 61 combat victories – 56 personal and 5 group – from the 122 air battles in which he fought. Rechkalov was awarded the HSU on two occasions, the first on 25 March 1943 when he was a senior lieutenant with 16.Gv.IAP and the second on 1 July 1944.

In postwar years, Rechkalov graduated from the Air Forces Academy in 1951 and by 1959 had become a Major-General of Aviation.

ALEKSANDR IVANOVICH POKRYSHKIN

To those in the west, Aleksandr Ivanovich Pokryshkin, is possibly the Soviet fighter pilot most easily recognised. Something of an enigma, he was a highly intelligent and outstanding fighter pilot, possessing a brilliant mind for tactics and astute leadership qualities. Pokryshkin was both loyal and outspoken, attributes which won him great respect from fellow pilots and the Soviet public at large, but emnity from political leaders, including Joseph Stalin.

Born on 6 March 1913 in Novonikolaevsk (now Novosibirsk), Pokryshkin joined the Soviet Army in 1932. The following year he grad-

uated from the Perm Air School for aviation technicians and, after a spell as a mechanic, a chance meeting with the great Soviet fighter pilot Suprun led to his attendence for flying training – Pokryshkin duly graduated from Kacha Air Force Pilots' School in 1939. During an operational career which saw him complete over 600 sorties, Pokryshkin took part in 156 air battles and was credited with 59 personal victories, although Ivanov Sultanov's (1993) Soviet-based account of VVS air aces credits him with 6 group kills in his final tally.

Pokryshkin's first operational mount was the MiG-3, and he later went on to fly lend-lease P-39 Airacobras with conspicuous success during the air war over the Kuban in 1943. His first taste of action was on the opening day of Operation *Barbarossa*, and he continued to serve throughout the GP War firstly as a deputy squadron leader, then squadron leader, assistant commander and eventually as commander of the 16.Gv.IAP. In May 1944 Pokryshkin was appointed to command 9.Gv.IAD, and he led the regiment in the massive air battles that became a feature of the fighting over both the Southern and Northern Caucasus Fronts, as well as on the 1st, 2nd, and 4th Ukrainian Fronts.

In 1948 'Sasha' Pokryshkin graduated from the Frunze Military Academy, followed some nine years later by a successful passing out from the General Staff Academy, whereupon he occupied several positions in the PVO (Air Defence Command).

Pokryshkin went on to fill the position of Deputy Commander in Chief of the National Air Defence Forces in the late 1960s, and in 1972 he was promoted to air marshal rank. In November 1981 Pokryshkin finally 'retired' from the frontline force to become an inspector advisor attached to the Ministry of Defence General Inspectorate. Four years leter, following a long illness, he passed away.

This unusual shot of the much photographed Aleksandr Pokryshkin shows him at the wheel of a lend-lease Willys Jeep. It appears that he had driven out to inspect the smouldering remains of one of his 59 aerial victories, which can be seen in the background (*Petrov*)

BORIS FROKTISTOVICH SAFONOV

As mentioned in the previous chapter, the first great Soviet fighter ace of the GP War was Boris Froktistovich Safonov, who later became the sole VVS fighter pilot to have a regiment named after him – an honour usually only afforded to great Soviet political leaders. The unit in question was 2.Gv.IAP, which had been Safonov's final command prior to his death in action on 30 May 1942 – the full title given to the regiment was 'The Pechenga, Red Banner, Safonov's Second Guards Fighter Aviation Regiment of the Air Force of the Northern Fleet'.

Boris Safonov is of particular interest to enthusiasts of RAF history, for he was one of the key Soviet pilots to liaise with British personnel during the handover of the first Hurricanes to the VVS during the early autumn of 1941. He had joined the Soviet air force at the age of 18 in 1933, and following the completion of his ab initio flying training, he enrolled in the Kacha military flying training school.

By 22 June 1941 Safonov had risen to become a squadron commander in the I-16-equipped 72.SmAP (Composite Aviation Regiment). He claimed the destruction of an enemy aircraft two days after the start of Operation *Barbarossa* when he downed a Ju 88 of 6./KG 30, which fell into the Bay of Kola – a loss subsequently confirmed by German sources. On 9 August Safonov was credited with the destruction of three enemy aircraft, at least one of which was a Ju 88. By 15 September his score had risen to 13, to which he added a further trio of victories during two sorties flown on this date.

During the autumn of 1941 the first of almost 3000 lend-lease Hurricanes were delivered to the VVS by the RAF's 151 Wing. Capt Safonov was duly chosen as one of four senior VVS Northern Fleet pilots (under the command of Gen A A Kuznetsov) to be taught to fly the Hurricane by RAF personnel at the aerodrome of Vayenga, near Murmansk. Remembered today by surviving RAF pilots as a high profile, photogenic, figure, Safonov played a significant role in instructing other Soviet pilots as they prepared for their first flights in the Hurricane. Although the lend-lease Hawker fighter was deemed obsolescent on the Channel Front, in the hands of an expert combat pilot like Safonov it became a superior gun platform when compared with the dominant VVS fighter of the time, the I-16.

Having completed his spell as an instructor, Safonov returned to action early in 1942 as the commander of one of the very first Guards fighter regiments. Formerly 526.IAP, VVS SF, the regiment became 2.Gv.IAP on 6 December 1941. Whilst at the head of this outfit Safonov continued to build-up a high personnel score, as well as serving as an inspiration to junior pilots – several of his proteges (including legless fighter pilot Z A Sorokin) went onto become aces themselves. On 17 May 1942 Safonov claimed to have shot down a Bf 109F of 6./JG 5 during a hectic air battle between the Hurricane IIBs of 2.Gv.IAP and the Messerschmitt fighters. His victim turned out to be 36-kill *Experten* Oberfeldwebel Will Pfraenger, who had bailed out and was captured.

Even on his last sortie Safonov continued to add to his score, his squadronmates stating that he had destroyed three Ju 88s from I./KG 30 prior to his P-40 being hit by return fire from one of the Junkers bombers,

This posed portrait of Maj Boris Safonov of 2.Gv.IAP VVS,SF, sees him climbing out of the cockpit of a P-40 not long before he was killed in action. It was taken sometime after he had helped liaise with the RAF's No 151 Wing in the autumn of 1941, during which time he had become only the second VVS pilot to covert onto Hurricanes. A double HSU winner, Safonov was the first great Soviet fighter ace of the GP War, achieving around 25 personal kills before being killed in a P-40 on 30 May 1942 (*Petrov*)

forcing the VVS ace to ditch into the sea. Boris Safonov, who is believed to had scored around 25 personal and 14 group kills, was never seen again. He subsequently became the first double HSU of the GP War, his second award being announced just two weeks after his death.

NIKOLAI DMITRIEVICH GULAYEV

Like Rechkalov and Pokryshkin, Nikolai Dmitrievich Gulayev was to achieve the bulk of his combat successes with the P-39 Airacobra, this pilot first coming to prominence over Stalingrad in 1942. He received the first of his two HSUs on 28 August 1943 whilst serving as a senior lieutenant, deputy squadron leader, with 27.IAP. On 5 March 1944, having since been promoted to squadron leader, Gulayev achieved the rare feat of 'making ace on a day' when he downed five enemy aircraft during the course of a single sortie. Indeed, March 1944 was to become a significant month for Gulayev for his personal tally also reached the 50 mark – by war's end he had scored 53 personal and 4 group kills.

Promoted to captain, squadron leader, within the 129.Gv.IAP soon after scoring his 'half-century', Gulayev received his second HSU award on 1 July 1944. Like most other successful VVS pilots, he pursued a military career in the postwar air force, attaining the rank of lieutenant general and becoming Head of VVS Operational Training – a post he held until 1976. Nikolai Gulayev passed away in October 1985.

KIRILL ALEKSANDROVICH YEVSTIGNEYEV

One of the 'magnificent seven' to score over 50 personal kills, Kirill Aleksandrovich Yevstigneyev was born in 1917 in the village of Khokhly, in Kugan Obl. He spent his initial military service working as a lathe operator at an aircraft repair base before learning to fly as a young KomSoMol at the Chelyabinsk Aeroclub, and then receiving military flying training at the Biisk Air Force Pilots' School. It was not until 1943 that Yevstigneyev commenced combat flying, joining 240.Gv.IAP (equipped with La-5s) shortly before they were committed to the Battle for Kursk – he was shot down and wounded during this pivotal action.

The La-5 was to remain Yestigneyev's mount throughout the GP War, the ace flying some 300 sorties in the Lavochkin fighter, during which he and was credited with 53 personal and 3 group victories. Prior to his temporary demise over Kursk, Yevstigneyev had downed eight enemy aircraft in just five days during June, including three Fw 190s, three Bf 109s, one Ju 87 and one Hs 129.

He was duly awarded the HSU on two occasions, the first whilst serving as a senior lieutenant, squadron leader with 240.IAP, and the second as a captain, squadron leader with 178.Gv.IAP. Yevstigneyev remained in military aviation postwar, and by 1984 he had become a Major-General of Aviation.

ALEKSANDR I KOLDUNOV

Just four short of the magical fifty mark was young ace Aleksandr I Koldunov, who qualified as a pilot from the Kacha Air Force Pilots' School in 1943 at the tender age of 20, and subsequently joined the Reserve Air Regiment. His operational career started in April of the following year flying Yak-1s with 17.VA on the 3rd Ukrainian Front. In

N D Gulayev, became the fourth highest scoring Allied fighter pilot of the war with 57 personal kills. This score was achieved whilst completing 240 sorties, although he only actually met the enemy on 69 occasions – a phenomenal strike rate. Included in his claims was a 'taran' on 14 August, 1943. Gulayev's first HSU award came on 28 September 1943 whilst serving as a senior lieutenant with 27.IAP and his second was announced on 1 July 1944, by which time he had become a captain with 66.Gv.IAP. (*St Petersburg State Archives of Photo, Phono and Cinematographic Records*)

August 1944 Koldunov became the first pilot within his regiment to fly the Yak-3, a type he was to subsequently enjoy considerable success with.

Although Koldunov had flown some 358 operational sorties by war's end, he had engaged the enemy just 96 times. However, he had left and indelible mark on the Luftwaffe, for he was credited with the personal destruction of 46 aircraft. Like most of the other top VVS aces, Koldunov was a double holder of the HSU, his first award being presented on 2 August 1944 whilst he was serving as a squadron leader with 866.IAP, and the second on 23 February 1948 whilst he was still holding down an identical position with the same regiment!

In postwar years Koldunov was to obtain high Air Rank, before suffering a disastrous, and humiliating, end to his career. After graduating firstly from the Air Force Academy in 1952 and then the General Staff Academy in 1960, Koldunov rose through the ranks to become the Commander in Chief of the Air Defence Command in 1978, followed by his appointment as Deputy Defence Minister. He was promoted yet again to the position of Chief Air Marshal in 1984, but Aleksandr Koldunov became the very public, and political, casualty of the daring May 1987 flight by 19-year-old Mathias Rust from Helsinki to Red Square, Moscow, in a Cessna 172. Despite having detected the German pilot early on in his unauthorized flight, Soviet Air Force authorities failed to act, and Koldunov was duly dismissed because of it.

VLADIMIR OREHKOV

As a 'typical' example of a lesser known Soviet ace, Vladimir Orekhov would have ranked about 200th in the overall VVS listing having achieved a total combined score of 21 personal and group kills.

He joined the Red Banner Flying School at Kacha in January 1939 at just 18 years of age, and by March 1940 he had graduated and was posted to the Ukraine. Upon his arrival Orekhov continued to fly a variety of training aircraft before completing a further 75 hours in the I-16. His personal aircraft ('33') was destroyed on the first day of the war, and for the next ten days, Orekhov and his fellow pilots tried to fly whatever machines were available, but such were the losses of equipment that those without allocated aircraft were sent to the reserve air regiment to collect new fighters.

It was at this point that he was posted to the newly-formed 434.IAP, whose two squadrons were equipped with the LaGG-3. Orekhov achieved some success with the new fighter, his first combat victory being over a Bf 109E which he bounced when taking off from Lyuban aerodrome – he went on to score a further three personal kills and one shared claim with this aircraft. By October 1941 Orekhov had been promoted to the rank of lieutenant and made a flight commander – on New Year's Day 1942 he was decorated with the Order of the Red Banner. In the spring of 1942 the squadron changed their LaGG-3s for Yak-1s, but Orekhov was severely injured in combat soon after when he was hit in the left arm and left leg by a burst of fire from an enemy aircraft. He returned to the unit just as the Yak-1s were replaced (in September 1942) by Yak-7Bs

In November 434.IAP became one of three squadrons within 32.GIAP (Guards Fighter Regiment), an honour which reflected the considerable success it had achieved during the battles of Kharkov and Stalingrad.

Considered an elite fighter regiment, 32.GIAP was commanded by Ivan Kleshchev, who had already been awarded the HSU – the unit moved to the Kalinin frontline sector soon after its formation.

In March 1943, 32.GIAP converted onto La-5FN fighters, Orekhov flying numbers '93' and '23' over the next 15 months, before re-equipping with the La-7 – he again flew an aircraft adorned with the number '23' for he was superstitious and always sought to fly a machine marked with a '3'. Orekhov was made a HSU in May 1943, by which time he had achieved 11 personal kills and 1 shared. His score stood at 19 personal victories, 2 shared destroyed, 4 aircraft destroyed on the ground and 2 observation balloons shot down by war's end.

In the postwar years, Orekhov continued to serve in the Soviet air force as a specialist in navigation, and by the time of his retirement and transfer to the reserve, he had become the Chief Navigation Officer of 1.GIAK of the Western Group of the Soviet Forces. Today he lives in Minsk.

IVAN IVANOVICH KLESHCHEV

Ivan Ivanovich Kleshchev was to achieve fame principally as the commanding officer of the highly successful 434.IAP – the regiment to which Vladimir Orekhov belonged. A veteran of the Khalkin-Gol conflict by the start of the GP War, 23-year-old Kleschchev initially saw considerable action over the Kalinin Front with 521.IAP, being recommended for the HSU in March 1942 as a result of his bravery. At the May Day celebrations of 1942, Kleshchev was thrust into the public eye as a result of an impassioned public appeal for greater resources to enable the fighter regiments to repel the German bombers. By this time he had 6 personal and 13 group kills to his credit.

Immediately after the speech Kleshchev was transferred to the Moscow to form 434.IAP, this regiment being the repository for some of the best fighter pilots that had survived the defence of the capital the previous winter. After training, 434.IAP took part in the defence of Stalingrad with its Yak-1s, the regiment acquitting itself well during the early summer. However, by July it had suffered heavy losses as its pilots struggled to counter the superior Bf 109G.

Falling just outside the top dozen VVS fighter aces of the GP War was La-7 pilot, and HSU, G Kostylev, who was credited with a total of 43 personal and 3 group kills. He achieved these victories during the course of 418 sorties, having tangled with the Luftwaffe on 112 occasions

Faced with annihilation, the regiment was quickly re-equipped with Yak-7s and it immediately started to redress the balance – as early as 15 July Kleshchev's regiment claimed 32 enemy aircraft destroyed for the loss of 3 of their own pilots and 7 aircraft in clashes over the Don river. By the time that 434.IAP was finally taken out of the frontline for recuperation and remustering onto Yak-9s, Maj Kleschchev's tally during the defence of Stalingrad had risen to 32 kills, although the split between personal and group kills is not certain.

434.IAP returned to action on 16 September 1942, but it was badly mauled just three days later when five pilots were lost and eight aircraft shot down, although the communists claimed to have destroyed 19 enemy aircraft in return. Kleschchev was flying one of the Yaks lost on this occasion, although he escaped without injury. He was not so lucky on 23 September, however, as he was forced to take to his paracute after being wounded in combat.

By November 1942 434.IAP had became part of 32.Gv.IAP, although by this stage Kleschchev had been temporarily replaced by Semyonov due to the former's injuries. Kleschchev finally returned to command 32.Gv.IAP the following month, but his return was short-lived for on New Year's Eve he was killed in a flying accident in poor weather whilst trying to fly to Moscow.

'LEGLESS WONDERS'

Like Douglas Bader of the RAF and Colin Hodgkinson of the Fleet Air Arm, the VVS RKKA had its share of successful fighter pilots who, following the amputation of their legs, flew with artificial limbs. A P Maresyev of 580.IAP had both legs amputated in March 1942, but subsequently continued his frontline career and scored 11 kills. Following injuries sustained in an engagement with a Bf 110, 2.Gv.IAP MiG-3 pilot Z A Sorokin received artificial legs and subsequently went on to score 13 kills. L Byelousov's case was slightly different from the others in that he had been severely injured in a pre-war flying accident but had managed to regain flying status, only to be injured again in another crash in December 1941. This second accident caused his old wounds to open, whereupon gangrene set in and both his legs had to be amputated. Drawing on amazing reserves of willpower, Byelousev again managed to return to operations, and went on to score seven kills. He was eventually awarded the HSU in 1957.

WOMEN FIGHTER PILOTS

586.IAP was the sole all-female fighter regiment to serve with the VVS RKKA during the GP War, becoming operational in April 1942 and going on to play a significant role in the defence of Stalingrad. In addition to this unit, female pilots were seconded for combat service with male fighter regiments (Klavdiya Nechayeva was sent to Kleschchev's 434.IAP, for example). Despite some considerable successes, no female fighter pilots received the HSU during the war, although postwar recognition was afforded to Lilya Litvyak.

Women fighter pilots faced an especially difficult task for not only were they accorded high publicity value by the Soviet propaganda machine, they also initially encountered scepticism and political interference from

This excellent Ministry of Information photograph, dated 8 January 1943, was captioned, 'Soviet woman fighter pilot shoots down Ju 88. Fighter pilot Lt Valerie Khomyakova, who brought down an enemy bomber in an aerial combat. Prior to her service in the Red Air Force, Lt Khomyakova was an engineer at the Frunze plant in Moscow, and concurrently worked as an instructor at an aeroclub'

their male counterparts. The record of Soviet women fighter pilots speaks volumes for their bravery and skill, however. Employed on largely defensive operations, the pilots of 586.IAP flew 4419 combat missions and achieved an aerial victory rate of 38 enemy aircraft in 125 aerial combats. The specific task of the regiment was to protect targets from attack by the Luftwaffe in the Stalingrad area, pilots being ordered to engage the enemy only when it meant defending the target – they were not to pursue the enemy after they had left the Stalingrad area.

Interviewed by former American WASP pilot Anna Noggle in 1994, Yekaterina Polunina, the regiment's archivist, gave an indication of the courage of the women pilots assigned to male fighter squadrons;

'Some eight crews from our regiment were assigned to two male fighter squadrons on the Stalingrad front, and they flew in pairs, with male pilots as their wingmen, because they did not have as much experience as the men.

'The wingman's duty was to protect the tail of the leader. When one of the girls, Nechayeva, was protecting the squadron commander, who was about to land, three Me 109s attacked them. She had no fuel or ammunition left, but she covered his aircraft with hers and everyone there saw her killed. Budanova, another of our pilots sent to the male squadron, perished in July 1943, but not before she downed over 20 aircraft, whilst Lilya Litvyak, who was also an ace, died the following month. Only five of the eight pilots sent to fight with the men came back to our regiment.'

LILYA LITVYAK

By the end of her brief life, Lilya Litvyak was to become one of great figures in the history of Soviet military aviation. Litvyak's mother was a shop worker and her father was employed on the state railway system. Neither were told by their teenage daughter that she was taking flying lessons at the tender age of 16. Eventually posted to Kherson for military flying training, Litvyak reputedly first went solo after only four hours of dual instruction on the Po-2 biplane trainer, and following graduation became an instructor. By the time of Operation *Barbarossa* Litvyak had accumulated over 100 flying hours, and she was eventually posted to 586.IAP as one of its founder members – her first operational air defence sorties were flown over Saratov in the summer of 1942.

In August she was posted for a few weeks to male fighter divisions and regiments – 268.IAD, then onto the La-5 equipped 437.IAP of 201.IAD. It was with the latter unit that Litvyak scored her first two combat kills during her second sortie with the regiment – a Bf 109 and Ju 88 on 13 September 1942. The former was reputedly flown by JG 3 pilot Leutnant Heinrich Graf von Einsiedel, a relative of Bismarck and a Luftwaffe *Experten* himself with 35 kills. Postwar studies have since shown that Graf von Einsiedel was probably killed some two weeks before Litvyak claimed her Bf 109. Her next claim was a Ju 88 on 27 September.

Litvyak's attachment to the female flight of 287.IAD led to a transfer to 9.Gv.IAP, which reached operational capability in November. However, political interference seems to have played a role in determining that Litvyak, as a woman fighter pilot, was not welcome as a member of this elite regiment, and a further (final) posting to 296.IAP was the result at the end of January 1943 – this unit was led by N I Baranov, who showed greater empathy to her plight.

Flying Yak-1s, Litvyak claimed the destruction of Ju 88 and a share in a Fw 190 on 11 February 1943, these successes being followed over the next five months a number of kills. Litvyak was herself injured on three occasions during this period of intense activity, the first time on 22 March (when she claimed a Ju 88), then on 16 and 18 July. Her great colleague, and female fighter pilot, Budanova, was killed on the latter date, and Litvyak's own luck soon ran out. On 1 August 1943, whilst flying her fourth, and final, sortie of the day (she had claimed the destruction of two enemy aircraft on this date), her Yak-1 was believed to have been attacked and shot down by Luftwaffe aircraft. There were no witnesses to the attack, and despite searches from Soviet ground forces at the time, no trace of her was found for many years.

In 1979 Litvyak's remains were finally found near the village of Dmitriyevka. She had been buried where she fell, beneath the wing of her aircraft. Some ten years later, and after considerable effort, her body was finally recovered for official burial. Lily Litvyak was posthumously awarded the Gold Star and the HSU by then President Mikhail Gorbachev in May 1990, although a monument had been created to her memory at Krasy Luch, in the Donetsk region, many years previously.

The Yak-1 of VVS 'glamour girl' Lilya Litvyak is refuelled in rediness for her next sortie in the late spring of 1943. As one of the leading women fighter pilots of the war, Litvyak had already scored at least 11 personal victories when she was killed in action on 1 August 1943

APPENDICES

VVS Organisational Structure during the GP War

From 1941, a Fighter Regiment (IAP) comprised three squadrons, which provided it with a nominal strength of 40 aircraft. Each squadron was divided into flights, or 'zveno' – during the early days following Operation *Barbarossa*, 'zveno' referred to tight, defensive, formations of three or four aircraft. A Fighter Aviation Division (IAD) consisted of three fighter regiments, giving a nominal strength of 120 aircraft, plus a further 4 replacement airframes.

Until May 1942 an Aviation Army Corp (IAK) comprised two or three Aviation Divisions of between 250-375 fighter aircraft in total. However, following Gen Alexsandr Novikov's direct influence, this changed from May 1942 with the formation of independent Air Armies (VAs) in place of the Aviation Army Corps, and these were comprised of five or more Fighter Aviation Divisions. Direction of the VAs was usually subordinated to the Front commanders, and by 1944 an Air Army could consist of well over 1000 aircraft, including fighter, bomber, ground attack and reconnaissance divisions. Seventeen separate VAs were formed during the course of the war, and these included fighter divisions.

Additionally, in early 1942 some 40 fighter regiments were allocated to air defence duties, and these came to form a new air arm – the IA PVO. By 1945 almost 100 fighter regiments were performing air defence duties, and these subsequently proved to be the antecedent of the Soviet fighter force in the Cold War.

Aside from the VVS, the Naval Air Forces also contributed to the victory in the east. An independent air arm since 1938, its forces were divided into four distinct air forces under the command of Lt Gen S F Zhavoronkov during the GP War. They were the Red Banner Baltic Fleet (VVS, KBF), the Northern Fleet (VVS, SF), the Black Sea Fleet (VVS, ChF) and the Pacific Fleet (VVS, TOF).

Lists of VVS Fighter Aces

As alluded to in chapter four, there are numerous inconsistencies in the lists of Soviet fighter aces produced during the postwar years. The most tables have been compiled by Sultanov (1993), Geust, Keskinen and Stenman (1993), von Hardesty (1982) and, most recently, Michleluc (1995). The top dozen pilots from each list are presented here for comparison – note that the total number of enemy aircraft destroyed as ascribed to each pilot includes both his personal and group victories.

	von Hardesty		Geust et al		Sultanov		Michulec	
	P	G	P	G	P	G	P	G
Kozhedub	62	0	62	0	62	0	62	0
Rechkalov	58	0	56	5	61	0	56	5
Pokryshkin	59	0	59	0	53	6	59	0
Gulayev	53	0	57	4	53	4	57	0
Yevstigneyev	52	0	53	3	53	3	53	3
Shutt	Not listed		Not listed		55	0	Not listed	
Glinka D B	50	0	50	0	50	0	50	0
Skomorokhov	Not listed	46	8	46	8	46	8	Not listed
Alelykhin	?	40	17	40	17	58	0	Not listed
Koldunov	Not listed	46	0	46	0	46	1	Not listed
Serov	Not listed	47	0	29	12	47	0	Not listed

Key

P – Personal e/a destroyed

G – Group, shared destruction of e/a

Michulec states that at least 310 Soviet pilots are accredited with 10 or more combat 'kills'. Sultanov concludes that there were 175 pilots with 25 or more combat victories, plus a further 140 that achieved 20-24 combat kills. It is reasonable to anticipate even larger numbers of pilots falling in the 10-19 combat victories category.

Aces by Total Scores, Missions and Enemy Contact and Strike Rate

Pilot	Total	Missions Flown	Enemy Contact		Strike Rate
Gulayev N D	57	240	69		1.21
Glinka D B	50	300	90		1.80
Kozhedub I N	62	330	120		1.94
Rechkalov G A	61	609	122		2.00
Koldunov A I	46	412	196		2.10
Yevstigneyev KA	56	300	120		2.14
Pokryshkin A I	59	600	156		2.64
Skomorokhov N M	54	605	143		2.65
Alelyukhin A V	57	600	258		4.52
Serov V G	47	not listed	not listed	not listed	not listed
Shutt, N K	55	not known	not known	not known	not known

Note: Gulayev's, Yestigneyev's and Glinka's strike rates cannont be determined with any degree of certainty as the number of sorties in which contact with the enemy was made is a minimum estimate. Even so, Dmitry Glinka is credited with achieving 10 kills in 15 sorties in the fierce air battle over the Kuban, and Kirill Yevstigneyev with 12 in only 9 sorties during the battle over Kursk.

Proportion of Kills Attributed to the top Aces

Top 10	- 450 kills
Top 20	- 897
Top 30	- 1348
Top 40	- 1761
Top 50	- 2148
Top 60	- 2507
Top 70	- 2843
Top 80	- 3159
Top 90	- 3461
Top 100	- 3752
Top 150	- 5124
Top 175	- 5759

In total, fighter pilots of the VVS claimed over 40,000 Luftwaffe and Finnish aircraft destroyed.

Heroes of the Soviet Union (HSU)

The Hero of the Soviet Union (Geroi Sovietskogo Soyuza, GSS) was awarded for the first time on 20 April 1934 to the seven Soviet pilots who rescued the crew of the research ship *Chelyuskin* in the Chukhotskoye Sea, north of the Bering Strait. During the Spanish Civil War, the conflicts in Manchuria and Mongolia and the Winter War with Finland, the HSU was awarded on 189 occasions, with four pilots receiving twice. Amongst this quartet was S P Denisov, commander of the VVS 'volunteer' fighter unit in Spain, who gained 13 victories during the civil war and was duly awarded the HSU on 4 July 1937. He received the award for the second time on 21 March 1940 at the end the Winter War, having led the 7 Army AF throughout the bloody campaign.

S I Gritsevets also won the HSU twice, primarily for scoring 30 personal and 7 group kills in Spain, followed by a further 12 in Khalkin-Gol. His second HSU was awarded on 29 August 1939, just three weeks before he lost his life in a flying accident. G P Kravchenko flew both in Manchuria and Mongolia, being awarded the HSU twice during 1939 for his exploits against the Japanese.

During the GP War, 895 fighter pilots were awarded the HSU, 26 receiving this award on three occasions, whilst Kozhedub and Pokryshkin became triple holders of the highly coveted honour. The status of the HSU was considerable as it was the highest military order the the Soviet Union could bestow, and it automatically brought with it the Order of Lenin.

Fighter pilots who achieved HSU status could expect substantial publicity, especially in their home village, town or city. For those pilots who received the award on two occasions, a momument in their honour would be erected in their home, and on occasion single HSU winners also had momuments erected in their honour or memory – one of the most notable was the great female ace Lilya Litvyak, who was belatedly, and posthumously, awarded the HSU in 1990. The momument to Litvyak is situated at Krasy Luch, in the Donetsk region. Finally, HSU winners would also have the award's five pointed gold star painted on the tail of their aircraft.

Double and Triple HSU Winners

Spain
S P Denisov
S I Gritsevets

Manchuria
G P Kravchenko

Mongolia
G P Kravchenko
S I Gritsevets

Winter War
S P Denisov

Great Patriotic War

1941
B F Safonov

1942
B F Safonov
V A Zajtsev
S Suprun (+)

1943
A V Alelykhin (x2)
S Amet-Khan
A Ye Borovykh
P Ya Golovachev
N D Gulayev
P M Kamozin
A T Karpov
A I Koldunov
I N Kozhedub (x2)
P S Kutakhov
M V Kuznetsov
V D Lavrinenkov
S D Lugansky

P A Pokryshev (x2)
A I Pokryshkin (x2)
V I Popkov
G A Rechkalov
A K Ryazanov
A S Smirnov
V A Zaijtsev

1944
N D Gulayev
P M Kamozin
A T Karpov
A F Klubov (+)
V D Lavrinenkov
S D Luganskiy
A I Pokryshkin
G A Rechkalov
Ye Ya Savitsky
I N Stepanenko
A V Vorozheiken (x2)
K A Yevstigneyev

1945
S Amet-Khan
A Ye Borovykh
P Ya Golovachev
P Ya Golovachev
A F Klubov (+)
I N Kozhedub
M V Kuznetsov
V I Popkov
A K Ryazanov
Ye Ya Savitsky
N M Skmorokhov (x2)
A S Smirnov
I N Stepanenko
K A Yevstigneyev

Key
+ - Posthumous

Notes:
- A I Koldunov got second HSU in 1948
- P S Kutakhov got second HSU in 1984

Guards Fighter Units

The honorary title 'Guards' carried considerable kudos for it was the ultimate recognition of a regiment's courage and achievement, thus setting it aside from other the mainstream fighter units. The first four fighter regiments to receive the title were 29, 526, 155 and 129 IAPs on 6 December 1941 – it was not unitl 1943 that Guards Fighter Divisions and Guards Fighter Corps were so entitled. Guards units were awarded a Guards banner, officers had the prefix 'Guards' incorporated into their ranks ('Guards Senior Lieutenant, for example) and other ranks wore Guards insignia on their uniforms.

Guards Fighter Aviation Corps (IAK) of the VVS KA

Original Corps	Guards Corps	Date awarded
1	1	8/3/43
7(PVO)	2	7/7/43
4	3	2/7/44
7	6	27/10/44

Guards Fighter Aviation Divisions (IAD) pf the VVS KA

Original Division	Guards Division	Date Awarded
220	1	31/1/43
102	2	31/3/43
210	3	18/3/43
274	4	17/3/43
239	5	17/3/43
268	6	17/3/43
209	7	1/5/43
217	8	1/5/43
216	9	16/6/43
210	10	25/8/43
207	11	25/8/43
203	12	not known
294	13	2/7/44
302	14	2/7/44
205	205	27/10/44

Guards Fighter Regiments of the VVS KA

Original regiment	Guards regiment	Date awarded
29.IAP	1	6/12/41
526.IAP	2	6/12/41
155.IAP	3	6/12/41
129.IAP	5	6/12/41
69.IAP	9	7/3/42
44.IAP PVO	11	7/3/42
20.IAP PVO	12	7/3/42
7.IAP	14	7/3/42
55.IAP	16	7/3/42
6.IAP PVO	18	7/3/42
145.IAP	19	7/3/42
147.IAP	20	7/3/42
38.IAP	21	3/5/42
26.IAP PVO	26	21/11/42
123.IAP PVO	27	21/11/42
153.IAP	28	21/11/42
154.IAP	29	21/11/42
180.IAP	30	21/11/42
273.IAP	31	21/11/42
434.IAP	32	21/11/42
629.IAP PVO	38	11/4/43
731.IAP PVO	39	11/4/43
131.IAP	40	8/2/43
40.IAP	41	8/2/43
8.IAP	42	8/2/43
512.IAP	53	8/2/43
237.IAP	54	8/2/43
581.IAP	55	8/2/43
520.IAP	56	8/2/43
36.IAP	57	8/2/43
69.IAP	63	not known
271.IAP	64	18/3/43

Original regiment	Guards regiment	Date awarded
653.IAP	65	18/3/43
875.IAP	66	18/3/43
436.IAP	67	not known
??.IAP	68	not known
169.IAP	69	not known
??.IAP	72	not known
296.IAP	73	3/5/43
572.IAP PVO	83	11/4/43
788.IAP PVO	84	11/4/43
83.IAP	85	not known
744.IAP	86	1/5/43
166.IAP	88	not known
??.IAP	89	not known
45.IAP	100	not known
84.IAP	101	not known
124.IAP PVO	102	7/7/43
158.IAP PVO	103	7/7/43
298.IAP	104	25/8/43
814.IAP	106	25/8/43
867.IAP	107	25/8/43
13.IAP	111	25/8/43
236.IAP	112	25/8/43
437.IAP	113	25/8/43
146.IAP	115	2/9/43
563.IAP	116	2/9/43
975.IAP	117	2/9/43
27.IAP	129	8/10/43
42.IAP	133	8/10/43
160.IAP	137	not known
20.IAP	139	not known
253.IAP PVO	145	9/10/43
487.IAP PVO	146	9/10/43
630.IAP PVO	147	9/10/43
910.IAP PVO	148	9/10/43
183.IAP	150	not known
??.IAP	151	not known
270.IAP	152	not known
??.IAP	153	not known
247.IAP	156	not known
??.IAP	157	not known
88.IAP	158	?/4/44
249.IAP	163	not known
19.IAP	176	19/8/44
193.IAP	177	not known
240.IAP	178	not known
297.IAP	179	not known
??.IAP	180	not known
239.IAP	181	not known
439.IAP	184	not known
??.IAP	211	not known
438.IAP	212	not known

A total of 18 Air Armies (VAs) were formed bewteen 1942-44, only one of which (18.VA) did not include fighter divisions in its initial complement. The purpose of the Air Armies was to ensure improved co-ordination of aviation divisions, which had previously been subordinated to either the Front Air Forces or the 16 Army Air Forces. VAs consisted of fighter, bomber, ground attack and long range divisions. In addition to the VAs, Air Defense Fighter Units (IA PVO) and the Naval Air Forces (VVS, VMF) were also formed.

Note that all kills quoted for each air ace represent the total kills credited throughout his/her operational career. In some cases pilots came to serve in more than one one Air Army)

1st Air Army

Established 5/5/42 on Western Front near Moscow
Initial Fighter Complement: 201, 202, 203, 235 IADs
Area of operations: Moscow, Rzhev-Vyazma 1943, Smolensk 1943/44, Byelorussia, Eastern Prussia 1944/45
Remarks: Top scoring aces of 1.VA included S Amet-Khan of 9.Gv.IAP, 6vIAD, on the 3rd Byelorussian Front, who was awarded a second HSU in June 1945 after 30 personal and 19 group kills. Also awarded a second HSU at the same time was P Ya Golovachev of 9.Gv.IAP, 303 IAD with 31 personal and 1 group kills. The French volunteer *Normandie-Niemen Groupe* flew with 1.VA, and included 4 HSU recipients amongst its 'foreign legion'

2nd Air Army

Established 5/42 on Bryansk front
Initial Fighter Complement: 205, 206, 207 IADs
Area of operations: Stalingrad 1942, Kursk 1943, Korsun-Shevchenovsky and L'vov Sandomir 1944, Czechoslovakia and Berlin 1945
Remarks: Several top scoring VVS aces flew with 2.VA. These included N D Gulayev (57 and 4) of 27.IAP, 205 IAD, 5 IAK on the Voronezh front during 1943; P M Kamozin (35 and 13) 66.Gv.IAP, 329 IAD on 2nd Byelorussian front in 1944; A F Klubov (31 and 19), 16.Gv.IAP, 9 Gv.IAD, 6 Gv.IAK on the 1st Ukrainian Front 1943; M V Kuznetsov (21 and 6), 106.Gv.IAP, 11 Gv.IAD over 4th Ukrainian Front 1945; V I Popkov (41) 5.Gv.IAP, 11 Gv.IAD, 2 Gv.Shak, 1st Ukrainian Front; and A V Vorozheikin (52) 728.IAP, 256 IAD, 5 IAK also on the 1st Ukrainian Front

3rd Air Army

Established 5/42 on Kalinin Front
Initial Fighter Complement: 209, 210, 256 IADs
Area of operations: South-west Moscow, Rzhev-Vyazma

offensive 1942/43, Demyansk pocket 1943, Smolensk 1943/44, Byelorussia 1944, Leningrad 1945
Remarks: Top aces included two double HSUs, A S Smirnov (34 and 15) of 28,Gv.IAP, 5 Gv.IAD, 11 IAK of the 1st Baltic Front, and A V Vorozheikin (52) 32.GvIAP, 3 Gv.IAD. 1 Gv.IAK, 1st Baltic Front, who had earlier flew with 2.VA

4th Air Army

Established 5/42 on Southern Front
Initial Fighter Complement: 216, 217, 229 IADs
Area of operations: Donbas and North Caucasus 1942, Krasnodar, Kerch, Kuban, Ukraine 1943, Byelorussia 1944, Eastern Prussia, Berlin 1945
Remarks: Aces included A I Pokryshkin (59 kills) of 16.Gv.IAP, 216 SAD (and subsequently 9 Gv.IAD); D B Glinka (50) 45.IAP, 216 SAD and then 100.Gv.IAP, 9 Gv.IAD; G A Rechkalov (56 and 5) 16.Gv.IAP, 216 SAD and also A K Ryazanov (31 and 16) of 4.IAP, 287 IAD, whose kills were all gained over the North Caucasus Front during 1943

5th Air Army

Established 5/42 on North Caucasus Front
Initial Fighter Complement: 236, 237, 265 IADs
Area of operations: North Caucasus 1942, Belgorod-Kharkov 1943, Ukraine 1944, Romania, Hungary, Czechoslovakia and Austria 1945
Remarks: Several double HSUs and top aces served with 5.VA. These included N D Gulayev (57 and 4) of 27.IAP, 205 IAD, 5 IAK on the 2nd Ukraine Front during 1944; P M Kamozin (35 and 13) 269.IAP, 236 IAD on North Caucasus Front 1943; I N Kozhedub (62) of 240.IAP, 302 IAD Stalingrad front 1943/44; S D Lugansky (36 and 6, plus 2 'tarans') of 270.IAP, 203 IAD, 1 ShAK, Stalingrad Front, and then with 12 Gv.IAD, 1 Gv.ShAK, on 2nd Ukrainian Front, 1943/44; G A Rechkalov (56 and 5) of 16.Gv.IAP, 9 Gv.IAD, 7 IAK on 2nd Ukrainian Front; and K A Yevstigneyev of 240.IAP, 302 IAD, 4 IAK and then 178.Gv.IAP, 14 Gv.IAD, 3 Gv.IAK, both over the 2nd Ukrainian Front during 1944/45

6th Air Army

Established 6/42 on North-Western Front
Initial Fighter Complement: 239, 240 IADs
Area of operations: Demyansk, Kalinin 1943, Byelorussia 1944, Poland and Vistula River 1944 and then onto the Air Corps of the Stavka Reserve in September 1944
Remarks: Aces included A S Smirnov (34 and 15) of 28.Gv.IAP, 5 GvIAD. 6.VA became the core of the reconstituted, and Soviet-directed, Polish Air Force

7th Air Army

Established 11/42 on Karelian Front
Initial Fighter Complement: 258, 259 IADs
Area of operations: Karelian Front 1942-44, Finnish border, Svir River 1944, before entering Air Corps of the Stavka Reserve by end of 1944

8th Air Army

Established 6/42 on South-Western Front
Initial Fighter Complement: 206, 220, 235, 268, 269 IADs
Area of operations: Poltava, Stalingrad, Donbas 1943, Ukraine 1944, L'vov-Sandomir operations 1944, southern Poland, Prague 1945
Remarks: Several key VVS aces including A I Pokryshkin (59) of 16.Gv.IAP, 9 Gv.IAD, 7 IAK on 1st Ukrainian Front 1944; Ye Ya Savitsky (22 and 2), Corps Commander of 3 IAK on 4th Ukrainian Front 1944; V D Lavrinenkov of 9.Gv.IAP, 268 IAD over Southern Front during 1943, and then with the same regiment over the 4th Ukrainian Front in 1944; A V Alelykhin (40 and 17) of 9.Gv.IAP, 6 Gv.IAD over Ukrainian Front and then Southern Front during 1943. Other significant aces included Amet-Khan, P Ya Golovyachev and A F Klubov

9th Air Army

Established 8/42 on Far Eastern Front
Initial Fighter Complement: 32, 249, 250 IADs
Area of operations: Throughout the Far-Eastern theatre

10th Air Army

Established 8/42 on Far Eastern Front
Initial Fighter Complement: 29 IAD
Area of operations: Throughout the Far-Eastern theatre

11th Air Army

Established 8/42 on Far Eastern Front
Initial Fighter Complement: 96 IAD
Area of operations: Throughout the Far-Eastern theatre

12th Air Army

Established 8/42 on Far Eastern Front
Initial Fighter Complement: 245, 246 IADs
Area of operations: Throughout the Far-Eastern theatre

13th Air Army

Established 11/42 on Leningrad Front
Initial Fighter Complement: 275 IAD
Area of operations: Leningrad and Ukraine 1943, Leningrad, Vyborg, Tallinn, and Estonia in 1944
Remarks: Top aces included double HSU P A Pokreyshev (22 and 7) of 154.IAP, then 159.IAP over the Leningrad. Front during 1943

14th Air Army

Established 6/42 on Volkhov Front
Initial Fighter Complement: 278, 279 IADs
Area of operations: Leningrad 1943/44, Baltic 1944 before entering Air Corps of the Stavka Reserve at the end of that year

15th Air Army

Established 7/42 on Brysank Front
Initial Fighter Complement: 286 IAD
Area of operations: Brysank Front 1942/43, Kursk 1943, Baltic 1943, Latvia 1944, Baltic Front 1945
Remarks: High scoring aces included I N Stepanenko (33 and 8) of 4.IAP, 185 IAD, 14 IAK on Brysank Front during 1943, and then with the same regiment over the 2nd Baltic Front in 1945; A K Ryazanov (31 and 16) also of 4.IAP over the 2nd Baltic Front 1945

16th Air Army

Established 8/42 at Stalingrad
Initial Fighter Complement: 220, 283 IADs
Area of operations: Stalingrad 1942/43, Kursk 1943, Ukraine and Eastern Byelorussia 1943/44, Poland 1944/45, Berlin 1945
Remarks: I N Kozhedub (62) of 176.Gv.IAP, 302 IAD over Byelorussian Front; A Ye Borovykh (32 and 14) of 157.IAP, 273 IAD, 6 IAK during 1943

17th Air Army

Established 11/42 on South-Western Front
Initial Fighter Complement: 282, 288 IADs
Area of operations: Stalingrad 1942, Kursk and Karkhov 1943, Ukraine 1943/44, Hungary, Austria and Czechoslovakia 1945

TOP 100 VVS ACES OF THE GREAT PATRIOTIC WAR

The following list is based upon the total of combined personal and group kills, giving wherever possible the number of operational sorties flown (Ops) and the air battles engaged (EA) in.

	Pilot	Total	Personal Victories	Group	Ops/EA
1	I N Kozhedub	62	62	0	330/120
2	G A Rechkalov	61	56	5	450/122
3	A I Pokryshkin	59	53	6	600/156
4	L L Shestakov	58	22	36	600/130
5	N D Gulayev	57	53	4	240/69
6	A V Alelykhin	57	40	17	601/258
7	K A Yevstigneyev	56	53	3	300/120
8	N K Shutt	55	55	0	not known
9	N M Skomorokho	54	46	8	605/143
10	I F Kuz'michev	54	18	36	not known
11	V A Zaitsev	53	34	19	427/163
12	M D Baranov	52	24	28	285/85+
13	D B Glinka	50	50	0	300/90
14	A F Klubov	50	31	19	475/95
15	P M Kamozin	49	36	13	not known
16	A S Smirnov	49	34	15	457/72
17	S Amet-Khan	49	30	19	603/150
18	V I Bobrov	49	30	19	not known
19	I I Kleshchev	48	16	32	not known
20	L Z Muravitsky	47	47	0	not known
21	A K Ryazanov	47	31	16	509/97
22	A E Borovykh	46	32	14	470/not known
23	A I Koldunov	46	46	0	412/96
24	G D Kostylev	46	43	3	418/112
25	V D Lavrinenkov	46	35	11	438/134
26	P A Pokryshev	46	38	8	282/50
27	I V Shmelev	45	29	16	not known
28	A I Belyasnikov	44	36	8	not known
29	S D Lugansky	43	37	6	390/not known
30	A V Kochetov	42	34	8	not known
31	P S Kutakhov	42	14	28	not known
32	S N Morgunov	42	not known	not known	not known
33	V I Popkov	42	41	1	513/117
34	A V Fedorov	42	24	18	464/104
35	A P Zaitsev	41	not known	not known	not known
36	I I Kobyletsky	41	15	26	not known
37	D A Kudymov	41	12	29	not known
38	V G Serov	41	29	12	not known
39	I N Stepanenko	41	33	8	414/118
40	P A Gnido	40	34	6	not known
41	V N Zalevtsky	40	17	23	not known
42	I V Bochkov	39	7	32	not known
43	V F Golubev	39	not known	not known	not known
44	I M Pilipenko	39	10	29	not known
45	A M Reshetov	39	35	4	not known
46	B F Safonov	39	25	14	234/34+
47	A F Solomatin	39	17	22	not known
48	M A Efimov	38	9	29	not known
49	M F Krasnov	38	32	6	not known
50	I I Babak	37	35	2	300+/103

88

	Pilot	Total	Personal Victories	Group	Ops/EA
51	A A Gubanov	37	28	9	not known
52	M E Pivovarov	37	not known	not known	not known
53	L A Gal'chenko	36	24	12	410/90
54	G K Gul'tyaev	36	not known	not known	not known
55	A G Dolgikh	36	not known	not known	500/97
56	A T Karpov	36	not known	not known	400/not known
57	N F Kuznetsov	36	not known	not known	not known
58	I A Lakeev	36	23	13	not known
59	N S Pavlushkin	35	not known	not known	not known
60	S G Glinkin	34	30	4	not known
61	S I Luk'yanov	34	not known	not known	not known
62	I N Sytov	34	not known	not known	not known
63	A M Chislov	34	not known	not known	not known
64	F M Chubukov	34	not known	not known	not known
65	V I Suvirov	34	26	8	not known
66	K F Fomchenko	34	8	26	not known
67	Yu I Gorokhov	33	23	10	not known
68	A I Kuznetsov	33	14	19	not known
69	N E Kutsenko	33	20	13	not known
70	N V Stroikov	33	18	15	not known
71	Ch K Bendelyanny	32	12	20	not known
72	M M Zelenkin	32	not known	not known	not known
73	V V Kirilyuk	32	not known	not known	321/75
74	M S Komel'kov	32	not known	not known	not known
75	V I Merkulov	32	29	3	not known
76	A V Chirkov	32	not known	not known	not known
77	A A Vil'yamson	31	25	6	382/66
78	B B Glinka	31	30	1	not known
79	P Ya Golovyachev	31	26	5	457/125
80	A S Kumanichkin	31	31	0	not known
81	S F Mashkovsky	31	14	17	not known
82	A S Khlobystov	31	7	24	not known
83	F F Arkhipenko	30	not known	not known	467/102
84	I D Likhobabin	30	not known	not known	not known
85	P Ya Likholetov	30	25	5	not known
86	V I Makarov	30	not known	not known	not known
87	S I Makovsky	30	27	3	not known
88	A A Mironenko	30	20	10	not known
89	S G Ridnyy	30	21	9	not known
90	A P Churilin	30	30	0	not known
91	V I Shishkin	30	not known	not known	not known
92	V N Barsukov	29	22	7	not known
93	A A Grachev	29	23	6	not knowN
94	P N Kiriya	29	not known	not known	not known
95	V A Knyazev	29	not known	not known	not known
96	I G Korolev	29	18	11	not known
97	I S Kravtsov	29	not known	not known	not known
98	I N Kulagin	29	24	5	not known
99	A F Lavrenov	29	22	7	not known
100	V A Merkushev	29	not known	not known	not known
	N A Naidenov	29	not known	not known	not known
	S M Novichkov	29	29	0	not known
	G D Onufrienko	29	not known	not known	405/not known
	M S Pogorelov	29	not known	not known	not known
	P A Pologov	29	29	not known	not known
	I G Romanenko	29	not known	not known	220/150

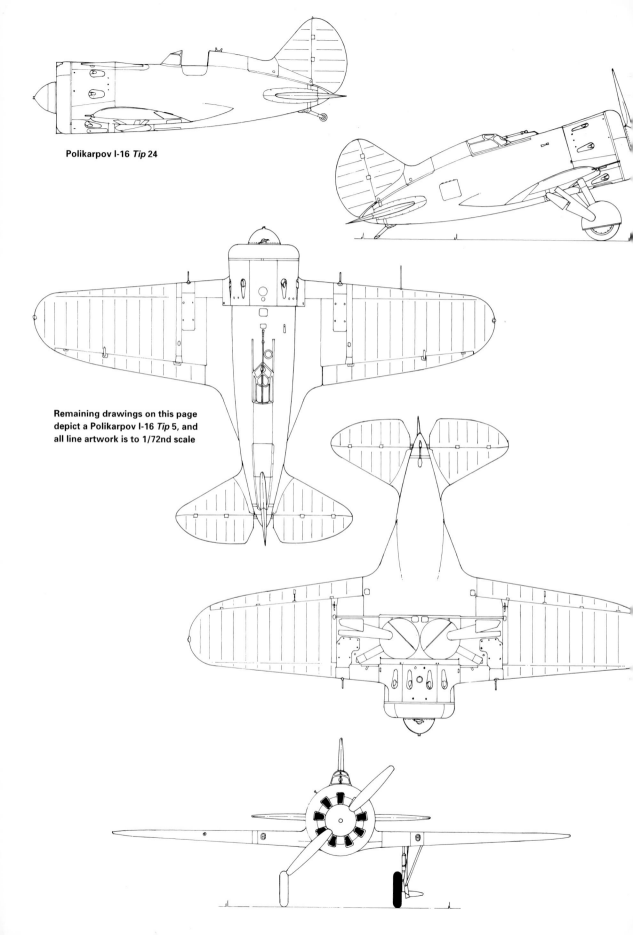

Polikarpov I-16 *Tip* 24

Remaining drawings on this page
depict a Polikarpov I-16 *Tip* 5, and
all line artwork is to 1/72nd scale

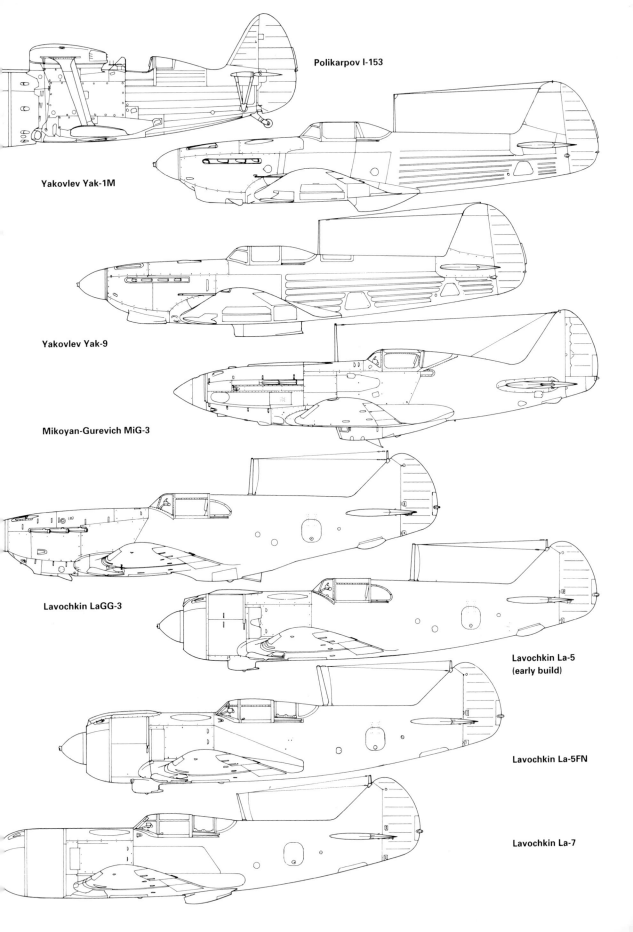

Polikarpov I-153

Yakovlev Yak-1M

Yakovlev Yak-9

Mikoyan-Gurevich MiG-3

Lavochkin LaGG-3

Lavochkin La-5
(early build)

Lavochkin La-5FN

Lavochkin La-7

Colour Plates

1

I-153 'White 50' flown by Capt A G Baturin, 71.IAP, KBF, Lavansaari, Gulf of Finland, Summer 1942

A nine-kill ace, Capt Baturin received the Gold Star of the Hero of the Soviet Union on 23 October 1942. His I-153 carried a red star on the fuselage but not on the tail, and was camouflaged in standard green and brown upper surfaces and light blue undersides.

2

I-153 'White 102' flown by Maj P I Biskup, Commanding Officer of 71.IAP, KBF, Lavansaari, Gulf of Finland, August 1942

71.IAP's I-153s were equipped with underwing racks to carry RS-82 rockets. Unguided projectiles were first tested by the VVS in Khalkin-Gol by I-16 fighters of 22.IAP, before being employed by I-153 regiments to attack ground targets during the 1939 Winter War with Finland. 71.IAP was eventually awarded Guards status, becoming 10.Gv.IAP, VVS, KBF on 31 May 1943.

3

I-153 'White 10' flown by Lt V Redko, unknown KBF regiment, Gulf of Finland area, September 1941

This I-153 carries the early style red star (thickly outlined in black, with inner circle also in black) and rudder numeral. Although this aircraft is fitted with underwing bomb shackles although no ordnance is shown here. The camouflage scheme applied at the time comprised olive green upper surfaces and light blue undersides.

4

I-153 'White 24' flown by Capt K V Solovyov of 71.IAP, KBF, Lavansaari, Gulf of Finland, August 1942

Like Maj Biskup's aircraft, Solovyov's I-153 is equipped with RS-82 rockets. It displays the red star on both its fuselage and tail, whilst the number '24' is located on the former only. Solovyov achieved ace status by gaining exactly five personal victories, for which he received the Golden Star of the HSU on 23 October 1942. His mortal glory was to be short-lived, however, for he was killed in action just 48 hours after Christmas Day 1942.

5

I-16 *Tip* 18 (mod) 'White 11' flown by Capt B F Safonov of 72.IAP, VVS, SF, Murmansk area, September 1941

Boris Safonov was the first great Soviet ace of the GP War, and by the time of his death in action on 30 May 1942, he had twice been awarded the HSU for amassing an estimated tally of 25 personal and 14 group kills. His I-16 was camouflaged in overall dark olive green upper surfaces and light blue undersides. The inscription along the fuselage reads 'For Stalin!'.

6

I-16 *Tip* 18 'White 13' flown by Lt S Surzhenko, 72.IAP, VVS, SF, Murmansk area, Summer 1941

The inscription on Surzhenko's I-16 proudly exclaims 'For USSR!', and like Safonov's aeroplane, the fighter is marked up with a black bordered red fuselage star. It is likely that the inscription and numeral on the rudder were painted in a grubby, and somewhat discoloured, shade of white which reflected the fraught state of hostilities in the aftermath of *Barbarossa*, rather than the fanciful reds, yellows or silvers employed by previous artists to depict this I-16 in other publications.

7

I-16 'White 16' flown by Snr Lt A G Lomokin of 21.IAP, KBF, Gulf of Finland, 1942

Anatoli Lomokin was awarded the HSU on 22 January 1944 and his I-16 was displayed in the Museum of Defence of Leningrad in 1945. He had enjoyed great success with the aircraft in 1942 whilst flying with 21.IAP's 8.MTAD (Mine Torpedo Aviation Division), this unit being primarily equipped with A-20G Boston, Il-4 and Pe-2 bombers. Whilst the latter attacked shipping and ports in the Gulf of Finland, the I-16s of 21.IAP would provide the fighter escort. During the latter part of 1942 the regiment replaced its venerable I-16s with Yak-1s and -7s, before finally receiving Yak-9s in early 1944. Lomokin remained in combat until he was killed in action escorting Pe-2s in his new Yak-9 in February 1944 – just three weeks after his HSU had been awarded on 22 January (it is likely that his HSU was recommended during the tail end of 1942, but was not awarded for over a year). During this time Lomokin had built up a distinguished record, completing 452 sorties, seeing aerial combat on 49 occasions and scoring 26 kills (7 personal and 19 group). The fuselage markings on Lomokin's I-16 were applied in white paint, thinly outlined with black, whilst an irregular size star was painted across the fin and rudder.

8

I-16 'White 28' flown by Snr Lt M Vasiliev of 4.IAP, VVS, KBF, Stalingrad Front, Spring 1942

This unit saw much action operating over the supply route between Lake Lagoda and the Stalingrad Front during the Spring of 1942. Vasiliev was posthumously awarded the HSU some five weeks after his death in action on 5 May 1942. His I-16 was camouflaged with dark green upper surfaces, onto which additional black-green patches had been oversprayed, and light blue undersides. This aeroplane appears to have been a sub-series 17 equipped with long-barrelled 20 mm ShVAK wing cannons.

9

MiG-3 'White 5' flown by A I Pokryskhin of 16.Gv.IAP, March 1942

Undoubtably the most influential VVS fighter tactician of the GP War, Aleksandr Pokryshkin flew the MiG-3 to good effect throughout the early stages of *Barbarossa*. This particular aircraft was an early-production model lacking an aerial mast and gun fairings above the engine. The cockpit canopy has also been removed, and camouflage comprising dark-green upper surfaces and light blue undersides applied. Note the underwing gun pack.

10

MiG-3 'White 67' flown by A I Pokryshkin, 16.Gv.IAP, 216 IAD, Southern Front, Summer 1942

This aeroplane was a late production model – note the different aerial mast and gun trough fairings above the engine. Like Pokryshkin's earlier mount, this MiG-3 had both fuselage and tail stars, a white fuselage numeral and spinner (as opposed to yellow). Camouflage is two-tone green and brown (A Pattern) on upper surfaces.

11

MiG-3 'White 04' flown by Capt S Polyakov of 7.IAP, Stalingrad Front, Summer 1941

This MiG-3 appears to have been a mid-series production model that had both the early gun arrangement but also an aerial mast. Polyakov's '04' had fuselage stars only, plus an off-white numeral. Camouflage shown is dark green with tan upper surfaces and light blue undersides.

12

MiG-3 'Black 7' flown by A V Shlopov, 6.IAP, 6 IAK PVO, Moscow, Winter 1941/42

The markings displayed on this aircraft comprised a red star on the fuselage, a red spinner and black numeral on the fin, plus a black arrow along the fuselage with the inscription 'For Stalin!'. The all-white winter finish to the upper surfaces was balanced by light blue undersides.

13

LaGG-3 'White 76' flown by L A Gal'chenko of 145.IAP, Karelian Front, Autumn 1941

Gal'chenko had achieved at least 7 kills by October 1941, going on to score 36 aerial victories by war's end – 24 of these were personal kills. This total placed him 53rd in the list of top scoring VVS pilots of the GP War. His LaGG-3 was an early production model that had a bulged gun fairing above the engine, a one piece exhaust manifold and upper and lower horn balances on the rudder. This aircraft was camouflaged in a non-standard two-tone khaki-brown pattern on the upper surfaces and standardised light blue undersides. The markings illustrated show no fuselage or tail stars (although a red star does appear on the propeller spinner), a white fuselage numeral and a similarly coloured personal motif on the fin and rudder which appears to be some kind of rodent (or even a cat) chasing a duckling!

14

LaGG-3 'Yellow 6' flown by G A Grigor'yev, 178.IAP, 6 IAK PVO Moscow, November/December 1941

Grigor'yev has been credited with at least 11 personal and 2 group kills, whilst his LaGG-3 shows 15 stars, indicating that he has perhaps been credited with less kills than he actually achieved. Grigor'yev's aircraft appears to be a mid-production model, showing three individual exhaust stubs and no gun fairing bulge above the engine, plus a re-designed rudder.

15

LaGG-3 'Red 30' flown by Capt S I Lvov, 3.Gv.IAP, Red Banner Baltic Fleet Air Force, Winter 1943

Lvov is another of those VVS aces who you would not normally see featured as his personal score was just six kills. However, he was clearly a 'team player', for he was credited with a further 22 group kills, thus placing him within the top 120 VVS fighter aces of the GP War. Lvov's LaGG-3 is a mid production model 35th Series, which was camouflaged with a heavily stained and weathered overall winter white finish on the upper surfaces and light blue undersides. Markings show a red fuselage numeral, red stars on the fuselage and tail – the latter only displays half the star, as the remaining portion has disappeared along with the fighter's original rudder.

16

LaGG-3 'White 43' flown by Lt Y Shchipov, 9.IAP, Black Sea Fleet Air Force, Black Sea, Spring 1944

Shchipov's LaGG-3 was a late production model denoted by its additional rear view glazing panel on the canopy frame. His aircraft has a white outlined red star on the fuselage and second national marking on the tailfin. A yellow unit marking lay across the fin and rudder, and a white numeral is painted on the fuselage. Shchipov's personal marking consisted of a lion's head on a heart, and eight kills were shown below the cockpit. Camouflage is dark green and tan upper surfaces with light blue undersides.

17

La-5 'White 15' flown by Capt G D Kostylev, 3.Gv.IAP, VVS, KBF, Leningrad, 1945

With a total of 46 combat kills, including 43 personal victories, Kostylev ranks high amongst any list of VVS aces, and certainly within the top 25. His kills were claimed during 418 sorties, having encountered the enemy on 118 of them. Kostylev was duly awarded the HSU, and in this profile his La-5 sports 42 kill markings, a small Gold Star and ribbon on the tailfin and the Guards emblem below the cockpit. Other markings include an elaborate 'shark's mouth', yellow spinner and rudder and white bordered Red Stars on the fuselage and tail.

18

La-5 'White 75' flown by I N Kozhedub of 240.IAP, 302 IAD, 5 VA, Leningrad Front, early 1944

The highest scoring Allied ace of World War 2 with 62 personal kills, Ivan Kozhedub flew a standard La-5 with 240.IAP (note that this was *not* a Guards regiment) which had red stars on the fuselage and tail, the white number 75 and the inscription 'Sqn Valery Chkalov' in honour of the famous pre-war Soviet pilot. Camouflage was dark green and black upper surfaces and light blue undersides.

19

La-5FN 'White 14' flown by I N Kozhedub, 240.IAP, 302 IAD, 5 VA, Leningrad Front, April-June 1944

One of only two fighter pilots to receive the Gold Star of the HSU on three occasions (the other was Pokryshkin), Kozhedub continued to fly operationally after the war. For example, during the Korean War he served as a member of the 'volunteer' Soviet presence based in China, commanding 324.IAD. The markings on this La-5FN are very interesting as they show the inscription 'Hero of the Soviet Union Lt Col N Konev' on the port side below the cockpit – the inscription on the starboard side ('From the collective farm worker Konev, Vasilya Viktorovicha') is the better known of the two, having often been illustrated in print over the years.

20

La-5FN 'White 15' flown by Capt P Ya Likholetov, 159.IAP, Leningrad, Summer 1944

Likholetov gained a total of 30 enemy kills, and whilst most lists credit him with 25 personal and 5 group victories, a recent table published in Russia states that he scored 30 personal kills but no group victories. Likholetov's La-5FN was a standard model, with white bordered red stars on the fuselage and tail, a white '15' on the fuselage and white spinner and rudder. The inscription 'For Vasek and Zhora' was in yellow, and FN is stencilled on the cowling. Camouflage appears to be the standard two-tone blue-grey on the upper surface with light blue undersides.

21

La-5FN 'White 93' flown by Snr Lt V Orekhov, 32.Gv.IAP, 3 Gv.IAD, 1 Gv.IAK, Kursk, July 1943

Vladimir Orehkov had been awarded the Gold Star of the Hero of the Soviet Union only weeks before the great Battle of Kursk, having achieved 11 kills mostly with Yaks, although his first claims back in 1941 were scored with the irksome LaGG-3. In the hands of an experienced combat pilot like Orekhov, the superb La-5FN was a potent gun platform, and the former went on to amass a further 10 kills by the end of the war. His La-5FN was marked with white bordered stars on the fuselage and tail, a white '93' on the fuselage, white diagonal stripes across the fin and tail, a red spinner and cowling ring, 14 small red stars indicating victory markings below the cockpit sill and, finally, the FN stencil on the cowling.

22

La-5FN 'White 01' flown Capt V I Popkov of 5.Gv.IAP, 11 Gv.IAD, 2 Gv.Shak, 1st Ukrainian Front, 1943

Popkov was a leading VVS ace of the GP War, his 41 personal and 1 group combat kills acquired from 513 operational sorties placing him 30th in the list of Red Air Force aces. A double HSU recipient, his La-5FN was camouflaged with standard two-tone grey on the upper surfaces and light blue undersides. Of interest from a markings perspective were the two white bands around the fuselage immediately aft of the cockpit, plus the 33 small red star victory credits over the bands and aircraft number. A large Guards badge can be seen on the engine cowling.

23

La-7 'White 27' flown by I N Kozhedub, Deputy CO of 176.Gv.IAP, 302 IAD, Germany, Spring 1945

Kozhedub flew a standard La-7 marked with white-bordered red stars on the fuselage and tail, red nose decorations and 62 white victory stars below the cockpit. At this stage in the war Kozhedub had 'only' two HSU awards, which were also displayed just below the canopy. His third Gold Star arrived (along with Pokryshkin's third) just after the end of the war in Europe.

24

La-7 'White 93' flown by Lt Col S F Dolgushin, 156.IAP, 215 IAD, 8 IAK, Germany, 1945

Dolgushin falls just outside the top 100 VVS aces of the GP War, and his aircraft is further illustrated in action on the front cover of this volume. Like Kozhedub, Dolgushin flew a standard La-7 camouflaged in blue-grey overall on the upper surfaces and light blue undersides. All 28 of his combat kills are marked on this aircraft, as is the Golden Star of the HSU.

25

La-7 'White 23' flown by Maj V Orekhov, 32.Gv.IAP, 3 Gv.IAD, 1 Gv.IAK, Latvia, September 1944

By this stage Orekhov had become CO of No 1 Sqn, 32 Guards Fighter Regiment, flying standard La-7s. His aeroplane was marked with white-bordered stars on the fuselage and tail, a white numeral, red nose cowling and spinners – 19 small red stars indicating victory markings complete the picture below the cockpit sill.

26

Yak-1 'White 1' flown by Snr Lt M D Baranov, 183.IAP, Summer 1942

Mikhayl Baranov has been propelled to prominence recently by Russian historians as his combined personal and group score of 52 (24 personal and 28 group) moves him into the top dozen VVS aces of the GP War. This previously overlooked pilot was both a prolific aerial marksman and fearless pilot, as the action on 6 August 1942 clearly proves. Flying in support of the defence of the Don River, Baranov led his flight in to attack an incoming Luftwaffe force of both fighters and dive-bombers, and during the ensuing melee, he shot down two Bf 109s and one Stuka before ramming another fighter after having run out of ammunition. Forced to bale out Baranov was injured and duly hospitalised for a short while – he was finally killed in January 1943 flying another Yak-1. Notable features of Baranov's earlier Yak include the camouflage scheme of dark green and black upper surfaces and light blue undersides, and the white inscription above the fuselage star which reads 'Death to Fascists'.

27

Yak-1 'White 50' flown by Lt Col V F Golubov, 18.Gv.IAP, Khationki, Spring 1943

A 39-kill ace with the Golden Star of the Hero of the Soviet Union, Golubov had his Yak-1 decorated with just a red star on the tail and a large white '50' on the fuselage. Again, an early Yak camouflage scheme of dark green and black upper surfaces with light blue undersides is seen on this fighter. Attached to Golubov's 18.Gv.IAP at around this time was the French volunteer *Normandie Groupe*.

28
Yak-1 'Yellow 44' flown by Lilya Litvyak of 296.IAP, Stalingrad, Spring 1943

The most famous female fighter pilot of all time, Litvyak was with 296.IAP when it became 73.Gv.IAP in May 1943. It was also to be her final operational unit, as she was killed in combat whilst flying with the Guards regiment on 1 August 1943. Litvyak flew a standard Yak-1 (complete with aerial mast) marked with fuselage and tail stars and a yellow, rather than dirty white, '44'. Litvyak was 22 years old when she died, and had scored at least 11 personal and 3 group kills prior to her demise.

29
Yak-1 'White 58' flown by Capt S D Lugansky, 270.IAP, 203 IAD, 2nd Ukrainian Front, November 1943

A leading ace with 37 personal and 6 group victories. plus 2 'tarans', Lugansky flew a modified Yak-1 with a cut down rear fuselage and all-round vision canopy. Camouflage was the standard blue-grey overall on the upper surfaces and light blue undersides. Included in Lugansky's markings is a white '32' nestled in a yellow wreath, indicating his personal score at the time.

30
Yak-1 (no number) flown by Maj A M Reshetov, 37.Gv.IAP, 6 Gv.IAD, 2nd Ukranian Front, 1943

Reshetov ranks 45th in the list of top VVS aces of the GP War, having achieved a total of 39 kills, 35 of which were personal victories. At the time he was recommended for the HSU he had scored 19 kills, 11 of which were personal victories. The HSU recommendation was often signed well in advance of the award being made, and it was not uncommon for there to be a gap of 12 to 18 months between the two events occurring. At the time of his recommendation, Reshtov had completed 432 operational sorties and engaged Luftwaffe aircraft 100 times. As with Lugansky's Yak-1, Reshetov flew a modified aircraft (note the absence of a radio mast), which was camouflaged with the early Yak scheme of dark green and black upper surfaces with light blue undersides.

31
Yak-1 (no number) flown by Maj B M Yeremin, 37.Gv.IAP, 6 Gv.IAD, 2nd Ukranian Front, early 1943

Yeremin flew in the same Guards Regiment as Reshetov, and like the latter, was also proposed for the HSU in 1943. However, unlike Reshetov, Yeremin did not receive his award until 5 May 1990, making him one of just a handful of VVS airmen to be made a HSU in recent years. The nomination for his award stemmed largely from his actions over the Taman region (near the Black Sea) in the early summer of 1943, when his regiment had fought a series of intense aerial bat-

tles with JG 52. Yeremin took part in 342 sorties, and engaged enemy aircraft on 70 separate occasions. He finished the war with 23 victories to his credit, 15 of which were personal kills.

32
Yak-7B 'White 31' flown by Snr Lt V Orekhov, 434.IAP, Stalingrad, September 1942

Sporting 434.IAP's unit marking of a red spinner and engine cowling, Vladimir Orehkov's standard Yak-7B is marked with five small red stars beneath the cockpit sill. When interviewed recently, Orekhov remarked that he preferred meeting the Fw 190 in combat rather than the Bf 109, as by this stage in the war he had had ample opportunity to test his mettle against the Messerschmitt, but not so the then new Focke-Wulf!

33
Yak-7B 'Yelow 33' flown by Maj P Pokryshev, 159.IAP, Leningrad Front, 1945

Having fought in the disastrous Winter War over Finland back in 1939/40 (where he was twice shot down), Petr Pokryshev gained a total of 46 kills during the GP War, 38 of which were personal victories. He received the Gold Star of the HSU on two occasions, the first on 10 February 1943 and the second whilst serving as the CO of 159.IAP over the Leningrad Front on 24 August 1944. At the end of the GP War, Pokryshev's aircraft was displayed in the Victory Hall of the Museum of the Defence of Leningrad.

34
Yak-9D 'White 22' flown by Maj M Grib, 6.Gv.IAP, VVS ChF (Black Sea Fleet Air Force), May 1944

Grib was CO No 3 Sqn of 6.GV.IAP, and his standard Yak-7D displays bold Guards and Red Banner badges on the nose and six small red stars above and around the tail star. Camouflage was standard two-tone blue-grey on the upper surfaces with light blue undersides.

35
Yak-9T 'White 38' flown by Snr Lt A I Vybornov of 728.IAP, 256 IAD, southern Poland, late 1944

Vybornov used his standard T-model (denoting that it was equipped with nose cannon) to great effect during the latter part of the war by scoring 28 victories – 19 personal and 9 group kills. He was awarded the Gold Star of the HSU in June 1945. Vybornov's aircraft is marked with white bordered 'Kremlin' stars (segmented dark red/light red) on the fuselage and tail and a white numeral on the fuselage, with 20 victory stars above. The inscription reads 'Pupil of Kashir'.

36
Yak-3 (no number) flown by Maj-Gen G Zakharov, 303 IAD, 1 VA, Lithuania, 1944

As commanding officer of 303 Fighter Aviation Division, Gen Zakharov flew a Yak-3 which displayed his personal emblem of a knight on horseback killing a Goebbels-faced serpent (a la 'George and the Dragon'!). This motif was superimposed on a white arrow/lightning flash along the fuselage, whilst a Red

Banner badge appeared on the nose. The standard Yak-3 was a particularly popular aircraft with regiments within 303 IAD, which itself never received Guards status. Zakharov was not only a veteran of the Spanish Civil War but also the conflicts in Manchuria and Mongolia.

37

Yak-3 'White 5' flown by R Sauvage, *Normandie-Niemen Groupe*, 303 IAD, 1 VA, German Baltic Coast, March 1945
Roger Sauvage ranks as the fifth-highest scoring ace of the *Normandie-Niemen* regiment with 14 claimed kills, although at least a further 8 have been retrospectively confirmed in postwar years. Of special note is the tricolour spinner (blue, white and red) and the 14 kill markings displayed behind the cockpit. Interestingly, the latter took the form of small German crosses in the custom of kill recording by pilots of the Western air forces – Soviet pilots refused to 'desecrate' their aircraft with enemy insignia, using small red stars instead. Camouflage was non-standard green and brown upper surfaces with light blue undersides.

38

P-39Q Airacobra 44-2547 flown by Capt G A Rechkalov, 16.Gv.IAP, 9 Gv.IAD, 5 VA, Ukrainian Front, Summer 1944
Double HSU Grigori Rechkalov ranks as the second highest scoring Allied fighter ace of World War 2, being credited with 61 kills – 56 of these were personal victories. Rechkalov's strike rate was also excellent, having achieved his kills in only 122 recorded air combats. Like virtually all otherAmerican-built lend-lease aircraft supplied to the VVS, this fighter has had the Soviet star superimposed on the former USAAF fuselage roundel. The P-39Q's remaining markings comprise a white 'RGA' on the aft fuselage, its USAAF serial on the tail in yellow, a red/white fin and rudder tip and 55 kill markings on the nose. Camouflage was the standard USAAF olive-drab and neutral grey.

39

P-400 Airacobra BX728 'Yellow 16' flown by Capt I V Bochkov, 19.Gv.IAP, East Karelia, 1942
Bochkov was one of the early VVS aces, quickly building a total score of 39 kills, which included 32 group victories. He was killed in action on 4 April 1943, and was posthumously awarded the HSU on the first day of the following month. Bochkov's P-400 (the designation of 'repossessed' Airacobras from the original RAF order) was camouflaged with standard RAF green-dark earth pattern on its upper surfaces and sky blue undersides. The smallish red star is superimposed on an overpainted RAF fuselage roundel, with a yellow '16' on the tail and a red tipped fin and rudder.

40

P-40K Warhawk 'White 23' flown by N F Kuznetsov, 436.IAP, Northern Fleet Air Force, circa 1942
Kuznetsov's Warhawk sports 14 white kill markings, and he subsequently achieved a total of 36 personal kills and was awarded the HSU on 1 May 1943. He flew a P-40K variant camouflaged in standard RAF colours.

FIGURE PLATES

1

Capt P J Likholetov of 159.IAP is seen in the summer of 1944 wearing a leather flying coat over his Red Army field uniform, of which the 'Gymastorka' (short blouse) is visible. His officer pattern belt has a side buckle, and on his head he is wearing a 'Pilotka' cap. In his hand, Likholetov holds a late pattern flying helmet and matching goggles.

2

Capt Boris F Safonov of 72.IAP within Northern Fleet Air Force, is seen clothed in an early-issue (there were several patterns) full length leather flying coat in September 1941 – essential wear when flying in an open-cockpit I-16. Safonov has a pre-war pattern fleece-lined flying helmet and goggles, plus an officers' pattern belt complete with a holster for his Tokarev 7.62 'T.T.' pistol. His outfit is completed by fleece-lined gloves, officer pattern boots and a 'single-seater' style parachute, all worn over his standard Soviet VVS service dress. On the collar of Safanov's tunic can be seen the rank patches of a captain in the VVS.

3

Capt A V Alelyukhin of 9.Gv.IAP in September 1943. He is wearing a two-piece leather flying suit, an early pattern helmet and officer-pattern boots all over his field uniform, together with heavy gloves and a 'single-seater' parachute.

4

Capt N A Zelenov of the 'Aviatsiya Voenno-morskogo flota' (VVS, VMF – Naval Air Forces) is seen in a black one-piece overall unique to naval pilots of this period. His helmet is early-style VVS issue, whilst his boots, gauntlets and belt are also standard air force faire circa. Zelenov became an ace flying P-40Ks in defence of northern Soviet ports in 1942/43.

5

Capt P I Chepinoga of 508.IAP in November 1944. He is wearing a service cap piped and banded with the branch colour of the VVS, and also adorned with standard Red Army officer cap badges. Chepinoga's service dress includes a 'Gymnastorka' blouse and breeches with officer's boots – he is holding his fur-lined flying helmet. The ace also sports shoulder-board insignia (branch colour, five stars and the winged propeller badge), which replaced collar tabs after 1942. Chepinoga's decorations include a Golden Star of the HSU, Order of Suvarov, Order of Lenin and Order of the Red Banner.

6

Capt I N Kozhedub of 176.Gv.IAP is seen in August 1944. His uniform details are essentially the same as for Chepinoga, with the exception that his shoulderboards are 'field' grade rather than the more formal 'parade' variety. Kozehdub wears a late pattern flying helmet, and is carrying gauntlets – his belt also boasts a Tokarev 7.62 mm T.T. pistol attached to it. His decorations include a single Gold Star of the HSU (he received his second later that year) and Order of Lenin.